Managing Child Sexual Abuse Cases

Of related interest

Boys: Sexual Abuse and Treatment
Anders Nyman and Börje Svensson
ISBN 1 85302 491 0 pb

Child Abuse and Child Abusers
Protection and Prevention
Edited by Lorraine Waterhouse
ISBN 1 85302 408 2 pb
ISBN 1 85302 133 4 hb

Child Welfare Services Developments in Law, Policy, Practice and Research
Edited by Malcolm Hill and Jane Aldgate
ISBN 1 85302 316 7 pb

Managing Child Sexual Abuse Cases

Brian Corby

Jessica Kingsley Publishers
London and Philadelphia

The right of Brian Corby to be identified as author of this work has been asserted by him in accordance with the Copyright, Designs and Patents Act 1988.

First published in the United Kingdom in 1998 by
Jessica Kingsley Publishers Ltd
116 Pentonville Road,
London N1 9JB, England
and
325 Chestnut Street,
Philadelphia, PA19106, USA

Copyright © 1998 Brian Corby

Library of Congress Cataloging in Publication Data
Corby, Brian
Managing child sexual abuse cases
1. Social work with children 2. Sexually abused children
I. Title
362. 7'6'8

British Library Cataloguing in Publication Data
A CIP catalogue record for this book is available from the British Library

ISBN 1 85302 593 3

Printed and Bound in Great Britain by
Athenaeum Press, Gateshead, Tyne and Wear

Contents

List of Tables

Acknowledgements

The research which forms the core of this book was originally devised in collaboration with Guy Mitchell, Mary Milton and Sue Ferguson. They helped to provide the impetus which led to the research being carried out in the first place, but I hasten to add that they should in no way be held responsible for the outcome! I am grateful for the cooperation and help given to me by all the professional people in the three areas studied who were generous in giving their time to be interviewed by me: social workers, senior social workers, child protection consultants and administrative staff in the three social services departments, as well as police officers, medical and health personnel, probation officers, education welfare officers and school teachers. I would also like to thank my colleagues, Malcolm Millar and Lee Young, for agreeing to let me use data from another research project which we carried out jointly. Finally, I would like to thank the University of Liverpool for providing a research grant to cover the costs incurred in carrying out this project.

Introduction

It is hard to believe the shift in thinking that has taken place with regard to child sexual abuse in Britain in the past decade and a half. In the late 1970s and early 1980s child sexual abuse was considered to be a rare phenomenon. It was associated in most people's minds with families which were grossly deprived and of low intelligence, often living in isolated (usually rural) communities. Child sexual abuse was almost synonymous with incest (Greenland 1958). The prevailing image of such abuse was of a father having an ongoing sexual relationship with an older daughter. While such behaviour was illegal and seen as unacceptable, little attention was paid to its impact on the child or young person and a view prevailed that it was probably best left alone. Fifteen years on, the picture is very different. Child sexual abuse is seen as a widespread phenomenon affecting at least one in ten children at some time during their childhood (LaFontaine 1988). The definition of abuse has broadened to incorporate all sexual activities between adults and children (including non-contact abuse) (Glaser and Frosh 1988). Practice-based research has shown that sexual abuse of children can start at a very young age (Hobbs and Wynne 1986; Macfarlane and Waterman 1986). There is now much greater awareness of the impact of sexual abuse on the victim/survivor, both in the short and long term (Beitchman *et al.* 1991, 1992; Finkelhor and associates 1986; Gomes-Schwartz, Horowitz and Cardarelli 1990), and, therefore, much less circumspection about the need for intervention.

Let me give you an example. In 1981 I was conducting a research project into the way in which child abuse was responded to by health, welfare and police professionals (see Corby 1987). It should be stressed that the term 'child abuse' was then almost solely equated with the physical abuse and neglect of children. The research involved observation of what were then termed 'non-accidental injury case conferences'. The second case conference that I attended took place in a residential special school on the outskirts of a large city in the North West of England. The main concern was about a 17-year-old boy who had physically assaulted his two young nieces while baby-sitting. His sister (the children's mother) had reported the matter to the social services department. The boy lived with another sister, her two children and his grandfather, and the main reason for calling the conference was to assess whether in the light of his alleged assault on his other two nieces, these two children (one of whom attended the special school) were at risk of physical ill-treatment from their young uncle. The referral also included an allegation that the sister with whom the 17-year-old lived had an incestuous relationship with her (and his) father and that the two children were products of this relationship. This allegation was not seen as the main cause for concern. Indeed, it seemed to cause a good deal of embarrassment because although the allegation pointed to a criminal offence being committed, it was clear that none of the professionals present felt that there was much they could do about it. The police officer said that it would take two months to process the case through the department of the Director of Public Prosecutions and the chances were that they were unlikely to prosecute. The phrase 'it would do more harm than good' was used. The head teacher of the school wanted to steer clear of the incest allegation as well. The chair of the conference, a female social worker who was later influential in developing awareness of child sexual abuse in the region, would have pushed it further had there been more general support for such action. There was no real consideration that the incest relationship might have been an abusive one for the mother of the two children. The prevailing view was that this was an established family and, despite its faults, it should not be disturbed. Indeed, it was argued by one member of the conference that you might find this type of relationship if you went into any house in the city!

Ten years later, as part of the research which forms the core of this book, I attended a similar type of conference which resulted from a referral from the Crown Court following a prosecution for incest. The 'family' involved consisted of a man in his 50s, his daughter (in her 30s) and their 12-year-old son. The man was found guilty of incest and was given a two-year suspended sentence and a probation order. He was advised to live away from his daughter, the incest victim/survivor, and the social services department was informed to ensure that the child of the relationship was adequately protected. The daughter had not initiated the prosecution and was not active in seeking separation from her father even after his conviction. It was thought at this stage that the relationship between father and daughter had not commenced until she was over 16 and that it was to a large degree a consensual one. However, the social worker who became involved with the family after the court case perceived very quickly that this woman was living in a coercive and highly abusive relationship and, despite uncertainty about the outcome for all the individuals involved, encouraged her to live independently with her son and to try to make a fresh start. As the social worker became more involved in the situation, his early perceptions were proved right. The sexual abuse of the daughter had commenced when she was aged seven and developed from there. It ended because the police saw fit to pursue a prosecution and the social worker encouraged the daughter to use this opportunity to break free (which she very readily took).

These two cases exemplify the major changes that have taken place in just over a decade. There has been a transition from very limited intervention to much more active and focused tackling of child sexual abuse cases. This transition has been a painful and difficult one for children (Roberts and Taylor 1993), non-abusing mothers (Hall and Lloyd 1993; Hooper 1992), abusing males (Morrison, Erooga and Beckett 1994) and all the professionals involved (O'Hagan 1989). Two major public inquiries at Cleveland (Butler-Sloss 1988) and the Orkneys (Clyde 1992) have taken place largely as a result of public disquiet and uncertainty about the investigation of child sexual abuse cases. There has been much debate and many heated arguments about the pace at which investigations should be carried out, about the manner of these investigations, about the roles of the different professionals, and about the rights of children and parents, to name but a few issues.

The main concern of this book is with the role played by local authority social workers in child sexual abuse work. This focus stems both from my own background and interests, and from the fact that social workers, while by no means the only professionals operating in this field, have key responsibilities throughout the spectrum of child sexual abuse work, from initial investigations to long-term involvement with children and families. They have key powers and duties in civil law to ensure that children are protected from harm. The responsibility that accompanies these powers is reflected in the fact that such social workers have also borne the brunt of the criticisms that have been made of child sexual abuse interventions.

My aim is to use data from a study carried out between 1989 and 1993 into 40 child sexual abuse cases investigated in three local authority areas in the North West region of England to analyse how social workers manage this challenging area of work. The intention is to examine both the context in which the child sexual abuse work is carried out and the intervention practice of social workers within this context. Much of the data is derived from social work sources – interviews with social workers and analysis of their child protection records. Clearly, this 'angle' is likely to have an influence on the findings. However, despite this and my own professional background, the intention is not to produce a social work apologia. Rather, it is to try and draw out from these cases which policies and practices seem to be effective (or ineffective) and why.

While there is much written about what social workers (and other professionals) do badly in the field of child sexual abuse work, particularly in inquiry reports, and a good deal written about good practice in more specialized settings (e.g. Furniss 1991), until recently there has been very little written (see, however, Wattam (1992) and Sharland *et al.* (1996)) about cases dealt with by the statutory authorities which are not the subject of major public concern. There is much that can be learned about key concerns and questions from a detailed analysis of such work. For instance, how constraining is the context in which social workers (and other child protection professionals) carry out child sexual abuse work? Do some social workers cope better with these constraints than others, and, if so, how? What are the qualities, knowledge and value bases that social workers use in this area of work? Which seem to contribute to more successful interventions and which do not? How effective is professional intervention in this field in respect of future protection and in helping children and non-abusing parents to overcome the impact of what has happened? How are abusing parents dealt with by the system?

The format of the book is as follows. Chapter 1 looks at broad contextual issues in relation to sexuality and sexual abuse, including societal views about sexuality and the contribution of sexologists. Chapter 2 looks at the recent history of state intervention into cases of child sexual abuse. Chapter 3 outlines the research methods employed in the study. Chapters 4 and 5 provide general data relating to the study sample. Chapter 6 looks in detail at early intervention work, and Chapter 7 looks at child protection conferences and planning longer-term intervention. Chapters 8 and 9 are concerned with follow-up work up to two years after the initial conferences, while Chapter 10 assesses the practice issues that arise from this study. Chapter 11 looks to the future and makes recommendations for policy and practice. Finally, there are two Appendices, the first giving brief details of all the cases researched and the second considering the views of parents at the receiving end of child sexual abuse investigations.

CHAPTER 1

History and Ideas

The aim of this and the following chapter is to provide a contextual backdrop to the study of modern-day efforts by the state to intervene into the sexual abuse of children within their own families. In this chapter, a brief historical overview from antiquity to the twentieth century is presented, reviewing how sexuality has been understood and regulated within societies, and in particular how the sexual treatment of children has been viewed and responded to. Chapter 2 considers the way in which current concerns about the sexual treatment of children have developed, first in the USA and then here in Britain, resulting in the forms of regulation that are in use today.

It has to be stressed from the outset that there is relatively little specific literature on children and their sexual treatment in history prior to the twentieth century. This has not been greatly redressed even now – as will be seen, this century has seen an explosion of writing about sex and sexuality in respect of adults, but very little attention has been paid to the sexuality of children and their sexual treatment (at least until the development of concerns about child sexual abuse in the last two decades).

It will be argued that, nevertheless, it is important to use what little knowledge there is about children and sexuality, and the much more extensive knowledge base about adult sexuality, to understand fully the social and political context in which current debates about child sexual abuse are taking place.

Before proceeding, however, it should be noted that much of the writing on sexuality has had little impact on those concerned with child sexual abuse in the recent era. The reason for this may be partly due to the fact that, as just pointed out, it does not dwell particularly on children, and partly due to the fact that, where it does, it does not pay much attention to the possibilities of abusive sexual behaviour towards children. As will be seen in Chapter 2, two of the key groups in modern-day responses to the sexual mistreatment of children have been child protectionists and feminists. For both, the involvement of children in sexual activity, particularly with those who are appreciably older, is considered unequivocally abusive. For child protectionists, such activity represents an abuse of adult power and exposes children to significant harm from which it is their duty, first and foremost, to provide protection. As a result they consider that issues relating to adult and childhood sexuality are not their primary concern. Feminists are equally convinced that adult–children sexual relations are abusive. Drawing on the fact that the vast majority of adults known to participate in sexual activity with children are male, they consider such behaviour to be a symptom of male power or patriarchy (see Dominelli 1986). They are highly critical of the notion that child sexual abuse may be linked to sexuality and consider that those who make this link both miss the point and run the risk of providing an excuse for such behaviour. Indeed writers such as Coveney *et al.* (1984) argue strongly that modern-day sexology is heavily influenced by patriarchal thinking and represents male perspectives on sexuality as being normal and essential.

As will become clear throughout this study, the issue of the relevance of theorizing about sexuality to state intervention into child sexual abuse remains a disputed matter. In the following review these issues will be borne in mind. The intention of the review is to sift out critically that which seems relevant from that which does not.

Ancient to Modern

The nature of human sexuality and its impact on human life has been a source of interest and confusion certainly from antiquity to the present day. Sexuality has been conceptualized and understood in a variety of ways, but an overarching concern, particularly up to the beginning of the twentieth century, has been how to reconcile what has been seen for the most part as a natural urge with the requirements of civilization and ordered social life.

The extent and the forms of this concern have varied between societies and over time but, as far as we know, most societies have been concerned to regulate sexuality in some way or other and this has been particularly true in regard to intrafamilial sexual activity or incest.

Greece and Rome

According to Foucault (1985, 1986), sexuality was less subject to overt control in classical society than in later Christian societies. In classical Greece, for instance, sexuality was seen as a natural quality and not as something shameful. Indeed the repression of naturalness/sexuality was considered to be potentially very harmful. This is most obviously seen in Euripides' *Bacchae* in which King Pentheus meets a terrible end as a result of his denial of the god Dionysus, who represents free-living/hedonism/sexuality (Kirk 1979). On the other hand, another Greek play, Aeschylus' *Agamemnon* (Fagles 1984), which depicts the vengeful acts of a woman whose husband has been unfaithful, shows the deadly effects of not adhering to some form of sexual regulation.

With regard to children and sexuality, it should be noted that extrafamilial paedophilia was an accepted practice in classical Greek society and was not considered abusive. However, it was largely a prerogative of the upper classes and was not as widespread as some commentators would have us believe. As will be seen throughout history, there is more tolerance/acceptance of sexual licence among the powerful than among other sectors of society. As for the victims of what we would now term extrafamilial sexual abuse, children and young people from poor and oppressed classes were those most likely to be at risk.

It is clear, therefore, that the Greeks did have social rules for sexual behaviour and that for the majority living in ancient Greek society these rules were not dissimilar to those operating today in our society. A key difference, however, was that there was no legislation and, therefore, no overt state intervention into matters of sexuality.

Intrafamilial sexual relationships, however, were of paramount concern to the Greeks. Sophocles' play, *Oedipus Rex*, is clear proof that in Greek society such relationships were seen as unacceptable (Stace 1987). Oedipus was abandoned at birth as a result of a prophecy that he would grow up to kill his father and marry his mother. He survived his abandonment to fulfil the prophecy unknowingly. When the truth of what he had done was revealed to him he blinded himself, and the kingdom over which he ruled was left to ruin. Other societies throughout history have created similar myths which warn of the perils of incest. Indeed social anthropologists have argued that the incest taboo is virtually universal.[1]

Classical Roman society viewed sexuality in a similar way to that of Greece, as an essential part of human nature and as a source of pleasure (see Wiedemann 1989), though paedophilia was not publicly approved of. It was not until much later, with the advent of Christianity, that any great emphasis was placed by the Romans on the distinction between body and soul which led to a polarization of sexuality and spirituality. Unlike the Greeks, the Romans did have laws

---

1 According to LaFontaine (1990, pp.31–38), incest is not regarded as a universal taboo by all anthropologists. Nevertheless, most societies have discouraged or outlawed sexual relations between close relatives (particularly parents and children) throughout recorded history.

relating to sexual behaviour, but these were practical measures designed to shore up family life at times when it was perceived to be under threat from licentious and uncontrolled sexual freedom.

Like the Greeks and virtually all other societies, the Romans also operated a strong incest taboo. This is demonstrated by Boswell's study of child abandonment in Roman and medieval European societies (Boswell 1990) which he undertook for the following reason: 'While collecting information about Christian sexual mores for a previous study, I came across the argument by several prominent theologians of the early church that men should not visit brothels or have recourse to prostitutes because in so doing they might unwittingly commit incest with a child they had abandoned' (p.3). This information led him to speculate on the extent and nature of child abandonment if such possibilities were thought to be that common. However, it is also evidence of the strength of the incest taboo in Roman/early Christian times.

This Cook's tour through the sexual mores of classical Greece and Rome demonstrates that the notion of the control of sexuality is not a modern one, but an issue for all societies past and present. However, what forms of sexual behaviour are controlled, by whom, for what reason and in what way all vary considerably over time and place. The exception to this is incest. The incest taboo (or various interpretations of it) is a highly consistent sexual rule over both time and place.[2]

Christianity and Sexuality

In Western Europe from the early Middle Ages through to the eighteenth century, sexuality came under the purview of the Christian Church, which acted as the state's moral arbiter (Gagnon and Parker 1995). (As will be seen, no secular laws on incest were passed in England until 1908.) Based on the belief of the spirituality of the soul within the human/animal body, notions of chastity and sexual abstinence were seen as examples of inner purity and sanctity, and the celibacy of priests was equated with holiness. Sexuality was considered to be a means of procreation and no more, and was, therefore, seen

---

2   Two further points should be borne in mind about the incest taboo, one regarding motive and the other regarding effectiveness. First, although incest has been depicted as an issue for all societies past and present, this does not necessarily mean that it has always been seen as child abuse. Indeed the concerns about incest have been centred more on family survival and genetic issues than on the feelings of, and the effects on, the child (see Arens 1986). Second, it should not be construed that the existence of incest taboos in antiquity or later meant that they were necessarily effective in preventing children from being abused by their relatives within families. Our current knowledge of the extent of intrafamilial child sexual abuse (see Chapter 2) certainly suggests that the taboo is frequently broken and there is no reason to believe that past societies differed greatly in this respect.

as an activity to be confined to, and contained by, the state of marriage. The Church became the manager of sexual mores by setting broad moral/sexual standards, and ecclesiastical courts were set up to deal with matters relating to the family and, therefore, sexuality. However, most of the work was carried out via the confessional. Sexual misdemeanours, including incest, were dealt with through one or other of these mechanisms. Punishments, or libations, were prescribed by the Church and administered through the priest. So, to use modern jargon, the Church carried out primary prevention work through the pulpit and the sermon, and managed the secondary and tertiary interventions through the confessionals, the courts and the ongoing work of the priests.

From the Reformation to the Twentieth Century

The Reformation led to a change in the nature of the control of the Church in a range of spheres, including sexuality. The notion of the Church as absolute arbiter was challenged, but its influence, particularly on the poorer classes, remained strong well into the nineteenth century. By the eighteenth century, more interest in sex as pleasure was developing, most notably among the middle classes (Weeks 1989).

The nineteenth century, particularly the Victorian era, saw a shift back to stronger moralistic views about sexuality. The middle classes placed considerable emphasis on the family as a source of moral socialization and rectitude. Officially, sexual licence was frowned upon, but prostitution and pornography, which had been prevalent in the previous era, continued to thrive. The public image and the private practices were at odds. Foucault (1979) saw the Victorian era not as one of repression, which is the popularly accepted view, but as an age where fascination with sex and issues relating to sexuality increased dramatically. He listed the following concerns which the Victorians had about sexual matters: a hysterization of women's bodies, a pedagogization of children's sex, a socialization of procreative behaviour and a psychiatrization of perverse pleasure (pp. 104–5). According to Foucault, this era laid the foundation for modern concerns about sexuality and shifted the locus of control of matters relating to sex from the Church to the medical profession – doctors became the new regulators of sexuality on behalf of the state.

Well founded though Foucault's views may have been about the hypocrisy of Victorian society over sexuality, the last 30 years of the nineteenth century were perhaps the first period in the modern Western world in which explicit concerns were expressed about children as victims of sexual crime. The focus at first was on extrafamilial abuse, such as child prostitution – a newsworthy (and salacious) subject (Gorham 1978). However, gradually attention began to be paid to the sexual abuse of children within their own families. The prime mover in this process was the NSPCC, which was formed to protect children at risk of physical abuse and neglect from their parents, but in the process of this work came across a large number of sexual abuse/incest cases (Behlmer 1982). This work was not particularly publicized and incest was seen as restricted to low-life families which lacked normal moral make-up (Wohl 1978). Nevertheless, sufficient impetus was created for the passing of the Incest Act in 1908.

In the USA, L. Gordon (1989) showed that between 1880 and 1910, the American equivalent of the NSPCC was also active in recognizing and responding to the sexual abuse of children. She estimated that about 10 per cent of caseloads were made up of cases involving child sexual abuse. Her accounts of early social work intervention into such cases are interesting because they show practitioners trying to make sense of what they saw as unacceptable practices by blaming poverty, ignorance, drink, inadequate mothers and the victims themselves in a way not too dissimilar, until more recently, from that of their modern-day counterparts.

Freud, Sexuality and Child Sexual Abuse

Sigmund Freud's work arose from this context, and proved significant for much of the first half of the twentieth century. His writing had a major impact on the development of thinking about sexuality in general and sexual abuse of children in particular. What differentiated Freud's views from those of his contemporaries was the primacy he attributed to the sexual instinct. He saw it as the main motivating life-force, influencing the shape of the human psyche and acting as the basic driving force behind all forms of human achievement. He argued that men and women were no different in this respect. For some these views were liberating and legitimated sexual freedom. However, Freud himself saw considerable conflict between the sexual drive and the demands of society. He was of the opinion that the sexual drive had to be harnessed and held back to meet the demands of civilization, culture and society, and that humans needed to control their libido and channel it into other areas (sublimation).

The development of Freud's thinking in relation to the issue of childhood sexuality and child sexual abuse has been well documented elsewhere (Masson 1984). Nevertheless, given its central importance to the history of child sexual abuse discovery, it is worth recounting briefly here. There is evidence that Freud was aware of the sexual abuse of children in the 1890s – he knew of the work of Tardieu, a doctor in Paris, who along with others was gathering considerable forensic evidence of such abuse. Freud at this time was of the view that childhood sexual abuse was a key factor in the development of hysteria in women (based on his experiences in clinical work). However, he later reformulated his ideas on the subject, and came to consider adult women's neuroses to be the result not of actual experiences of sexual abuse, as their accounts suggested, but of repression of their instinctive sexuality. A classic example of this line of thinking is to be found in his account of the case of Dora (Decker 1981, 1991; Masson 1989).[3] As his theory of psycho-sexual development evolved, Freud also formed the idea that accounts of childhood sexual abuse by adults could be fantasies or wish fulfilments rather than reality, a view that is currently being raised again under the title of false memory syndrome (see Schuman and Galvez 1996).

With hindsight, Freud's legacy has been a mixed one. He contributed considerably to the awareness and understanding of childhood sexuality and sexuality in general, though many feminist writers would dispute this in the case regarding women (see Sydie 1987). However, his theory of psycho-sexual development in children had the effect of reducing the likelihood that those who alleged that they had been sexually abused as children would be believed by medical and other professionals. To this extent it could be argued that he delayed, or, at the least, failed to expedite, the 'discovery' of child sexual abuse for over half a century.

---

3   These accounts make fascinating reading in terms of understanding the extent to which Freud's ideas on sexuality and sexual abuse, despite being seen as revolutionary, were rooted in the social context in which he lived. They also demonstrate clearly how this type of thinking, despite offering the possibility of opening up the problem of child sexual abuse, in fact served only to push it further back into the shadows. The brief facts of the case of Dora are as follows. At the age of 18, she was brought to Freud by her father because she was depressed and her character had changed. The problems were said to have started two years earlier when she alleged to her mother that a friend of her father had made sexual advances to her. He had denied the incident and the father had believed him. During her sessions with Freud, it was revealed that Dora had suffered from physical anxiety symptoms from the age of 8, that her father had contracted syphilis when she was 12, that her father's friend (Herr K) had previously made sexual advances to her when she was 14, and that her father was having an affair with his friend's wife (Frau K). Freud's diagnosis of the situation was that Dora's problems were (1) that she had sexual wish fulfilments for her father (faulty psycho-sexual development) and (2) that she had been sexually aroused by the advances made to her by Herr K when she was 14, but could not allow herself consciously to accept these feelings and the effect of their repression had brought about her depressed state and difficult behaviour! On the credit side, Freud did believe that Dora had been sexually propositioned by Herr K. However, there is no evidence that he suspected that Dora might have been sexually abused by her father at an earlier age. Decker (1981) describes Freud's remedy as follows: 'First of all, the only changes Freud believed he ought to bring about were to rid Dora of her various hysterical symptoms by making her aware, through appropriate psychoanalytic techniques, of her unconscious fantasies and desires regarding her father, Herr K. and Frau K. ... If any course of action were preferable, it was that the K.'s should get divorced, so Dora could marry Herr K.: "the scheme would by no means have been so impracticable," Freud told Dora. "This would have been the best possible solution for all parties concerned"' (pp.447–448).

Twentieth Century Sexology

Freud could be considered the first of the sexologists; there was a deluge of them to follow. The twentieth century is littered with texts on sexuality. Extensive studies of sexual behaviour have been carried out by Ellis (1913), Kinsey *et al.* (1948, 1953), Masters and Johnson (1966, 1970) (all of whose work has been very well summarized and analysed by Robinson 1976) and, finally, Hite (1976, 1981). Gagnon and Parker (1995) describe the period between 1890 and 1980 as the sexological period in the history of sexuality, a time in which concerted efforts were made to create a science of sexuality, as if to harness it once and for all.

The focus of much of what was written during this period was on gathering information about and understanding sexual practices. Much of the writing was less negative about sex and sexuality than the work of Freud. Most of the sexologists writing in this era were, within the limits of their time, liberators. Ellis (1913), for instance, saw sexual behaviour as healthy, not to be repressed. Kinsey and his colleagues (1948, 1953) were of the view that empirical studies of sexual behaviour would provide the key to the understanding of sexuality. Accordingly they conducted 18,000 interviews in the period between 1938 and 1956. Like Ellis, they came to the conclusion that sexual variety was normal (and, therefore, desirable).

Despite this opening up of sexuality and the liberal attitudes that accompanied it, the focus was very much on adult sexuality and, as Coveney *et al.* (1984) convincingly argue, on adult male sexuality. Ellis had almost nothing to say about childhood sexuality. Kinsey and his colleagues provided some material. They found that half of the males in their studies were involved in pre-adolescent sex play and many achieved orgasms between the ages of 7 and 12. Kinsey and his colleagues were, therefore, of the view that childhood sexuality was normal and not to be discouraged. They dismissed the theory of latency put forward by Freud. As far as they were concerned, sexual behaviour and activity, left to its own devices, existed throughout childhood and indeed reached its peak in adolescence.

However, in their desire to liberate sexuality, Kinsey and his co-researchers seem to have ignored the possibilities of child sexual abuse. For instance, 9 males interviewed gave information about the sexual capacities of 317 pre-adolescents, a finding which was not viewed as a reason for suspicion! A quarter of female respondents in their study of female sexuality reported that they had been approached sexually during childhood by a man at least five years older than them. Again, these revelations were not seen as either significant or as a cause for concern. Indeed Kinsey and his colleagues seemed to suggest that child molestation was grossly exaggerated: 'Many small girls reflect the public hysteria over the prospect of "being touched" by a strange person; and many a child, who has no idea of the mechanics of intercourse, interprets affection and simple caressing, from anyone except her own parents, as attempts at rape' (1948, p.238). According to Robinson (1976)

> Only a small portion of the sexual approaches made to children, Kinsey found, eventuated in actual physical contact, and if those approaches sometimes caused psychological damage, that was to be attributed to cultural conditioning rather than to anything pathogenic in the experience itself. Indeed he was brazen enough to suggest that children sometimes enjoyed their sexual encounters with adults. (p.92)[4]

Interestingly, no reference is made to intrafamilial child sexual relationships by Kinsey – one shudders to think what he would have made of them.

Masters and Johnson (1966, 1970) have very little to say about younger people. Their studies focused largely on the physiology of sex, the quality of sexual relationships within marriage and how to improve that quality.

Hite (1976, 1981) is less concerned with the mechanics of sex and more with the emotions. Her work is based on accounts by women of their sexual experiences and needs. This is the first of the survey studies that looks at sexuality from a female point of view. However, Hite's survey is no different from the rest when it comes to the issue of childhood sexuality or sexual abuse – there is very little comment.

Sexual Liberation

The net impact of these various sexological studies and writings was to enhance an atmosphere of sexual liberation which took place in Western societies in the 1960s and 1970s. Achieving sexual gratification was placed on a pedestal; casual sex (aided by the advent of the Pill) was tolerated/ encouraged; homosexual relationships between consenting male adults over 21 was belatedly legalized. Sex became both fun and *de rigueur.* It was brought more into the open but was still viewed with considerable ambivalence, as demonstrated by the Profumo affair and the trial of Lawrence's *Lady Chatterley's Lover.* With regard to childhood sexuality, the new spirit of liberation gave some legitimacy to societies such as the Paedophile Information Exchange in Britain and the Rene Guyon Society in the USA which wished to legalize

4   That the dearth of knowledge about childhood sexuality continues to exist is confirmed by Vizard, Monck and Misch (1995). In their review they found only one large-scale study of sexual behaviour in 'normal' children – by Friedrich *et al.* (1991). Vizard and her colleagues clearly demonstrate how this gap in our knowledge and understanding hinders in particular the development of programmes for working with child and adolescent sex offenders.

adult/child relationships. The scene began to change in the early 1980s as a result of a variety of different influences: the advent of AIDS, the rise of a strong feminist movement and the championing of the family by the Thatcher administration.

The Modern Construction of Sexuality

The theorizing of sexuality also shifted in the 1980s and 1990s. Writers such as Kinsey and Masters and Johnson saw the sexual drive as an essential quality of human nature which needed to be liberated from the shackles of society. Theorists in the last decade-and-a-half have focused much more on how sexuality is socially constructed, placing far less emphasis on its biological base. Foucault's work has been a major influence in this shift. His view was that sex and sexuality were areas of existence through which control could be most powerfully established over human behaviour – hence society's preoccupation with the topic. He argued that there was no such thing as a sexuality, but that the idea of one was being used as a mechanism of societal control. In the words of Mcnay, Foucault's message was that 'the introspective search for a hidden essence prevents individuals from recognising the essentially "constructed" nature of their sexuality and, hence, from seeing the potentiality for change and experimentation' (Mcnay 1994, p.98). If one ignores the society-as-conspirator implications of this, there is an important message about how people's sexuality can be defined for them rather than them shaping it for themselves. A postmodern view is that there are many sexualities and that they all have validity in their own right. As a result, we cannot afford to make sweeping transcultural and transhistorical generalizations about the nature of sexuality (see Weeks 1995). However, the same criticism applies to current sexologists as to those in the past: despite paying attention to a broader spectrum of sexual issues than their predecessors – including race, gender and different sexual orientations – they too make little reference to childhood sexuality. In addition they make no comment about the problem that the notion of multiple sexualities avoids the thorny issue of sexual relationships between children and adults. This is particularly surprising given that child sexual abuse has been on the public agenda in Britain since the early 1980s and in the USA from even earlier. The lack of attention from this quarter represents a major deficit in our understanding of the issue of child sexual abuse.

Regulating Child Sexual Abuse

It was pointed out at the beginning of this chapter that child sexual abuse has mainly been 'discovered' in the modern era by professionals whose concern is child protection (Kempe 1978). A major impact has been made on the issue by feminist professionals and writers (see Rush 1980). A third element with considerable influence in this field is the fact that, particularly in Britain, child sexual abuse has been seen primarily as a crime (see West 1987). These influences on the regulation of child sexual abuse have been positive in many respects – they have ensured that abuse allegations are taken seriously; they have ensured that children are not blamed for what has happened to them; they have ensured that future protection needs are prioritized. However, those working from these perspectives have tended to place little emphasis on sex and sexuality, and in the case of the feminist perspective there has been downright hostility to such a notion. There are, however, some weaknesses created by the lack of consideration of sexuality and society's attitudes to sexuality when dealing with child sexual abuse. For instance, there are dangers of crude interventionism if the theoretical underpinnings are relatively simp-listic and narrow (see Stewart 1996). Greater understanding of issues of sex and sexuality might enable professionals in this field to develop a more detached awareness of their roles and functions. Similarly, greater knowledge of adult sexual behaviour, drawing on the work of sexologists, might improve the ability of professionals to cope better with the subject matter of their in-vestigations. Except for those who specialize in sexual therapy or work with sexual offenders, most professional child protection workers tend to share the problems (and ignorance) of the majority of people in society with regard to sex and sexuality (see Davies 1983; Milner 1986). They are simply not comfortable with the topic. This could be remedied. As we have seen, however, the writing on sexuality does not offer much encouragement in this respect, most notably evidenced by a lack of attention given to issues relating to children and, at least until most recently, by a predominance of the male perspective. This writing must, therefore, be used in a critical and informed way. What is clearly needed is much more objective research on child sexuality and related issues. These matters will be returned to in the concluding chapter.

Summary

The aim of this short survey has been to examine how societies have throughout recorded history regulated sexuality. In particular it has considered the relevance of sexuality theorists (or sexologists) to the issue of child sexual abuse in the modern era. The general conclusion reached is that researchers and writers in this field have had very little to say about childhood sexuality and adult/child sexual relationships. Those that have addressed the topic, Freud and Kinsey in particular, have glossed over the issue and have been dismissive of the notion of child sexual abuse. Given the nature of theorizing about sexuality and the lack of consideration given to children by sex experts, it is perhaps not surprising that child protection professionals have derived their theoretical guidance from other sources. This is seen as a deficit in that greater understanding and awareness of sexual issues relating to both adults and children could make important contributions to professional interventions into child sexual abuse cases.

CHAPTER 2

Developing a Response to Child Sexual Abuse

As has been seen in the previous chapter, the notion of child sexual abuse prompted solely by concern for the well-being of children arose first in late Victorian times. However, intrafamilial child sexual abuse did not develop as a major societal issue for another 70 to 80 years. Incest, though a criminal offence in Britain from 1908, continued to be seen as a practice associated with low-life, deprived and isolated families. Prosecutions for incest after the passing of the Act remained under a hundred per year until the end of the Second World War and rose only slowly until the mid-1980s, by when the yearly total had increased sharply to 500. As demonstrated in the Introduction to this book, even as late as the end of the 1970s, child sexual abuse was still seen as a rare occurrence of little public concern.

The Modern-day Response – USA

Across the Atlantic, however, a major shift was taking place at this time. A combination of influences and concerns led to child sexual abuse being firmly established on the social policy agenda by the end of the 1970s (see Olafson, Corwin and Summit 1993).

Child Protectionists

The first of these influences was the impact of the child protectionist lobby. Henry Kempe, a paediatrician, and his colleagues had been very successful in bringing physical abuse and neglect of children to the attention of the public (Helfer and Kempe 1968; Kempe *et al.* 1962). By 1974 the Child Abuse, Prevention and Treatment Act had been passed, making it obligatory for professionals to report incidents of child abuse and for child protection agencies to follow up these reports and provide help and treatment to children (see Fraser 1976). Although this piece of legislation was framed with physical abuse and neglect in mind, knowledge and awareness of child sexual abuse was being demonstrated by the medical and social work professions in the mid-1970s, as demonstrated by Schechter and Roberge (1976). The philosophy of the child protectionist lobby was that sexual activities between adults and children were abusive because they were not natural and were damaging to the psychological and sexual development of children (see Kempe 1978). Finkelhor, writing in 1979, added a further moral dimension of a kind totally lacking from the literature reviewed in the previous chapter: 'The basic proposition here is that adult–child sex is wrong because the fundamental conditions of consent cannot prevail in the relationship between an adult and a child' (Finkelhor 1979a, p.695). He argued that children could not give informed consent to sexual relations, first because they were generally ignorant about sex and sexuality, and second, because they were almost totally subject to adult rules and influence. Keenly aware of the views of sexual liberationists, Finkelhor considered it of prime importance that the ethical arguments against child–adult sexual relations be voiced: 'Concern about sexual abuse of children is not part of a Victorian resurgence. It is compatible with the most progressive attitude towards sexuality currently being voiced, a position that urges that consent be the sole standard by which the legitimacy of sexual acts be evaluated' (p.697).

Family-based Concerns

The second influence came from those whose focus was more on the impact of child sexual abuse on the family. Giaretto's emphasis was on finding ways of helping families to cope with the effect of the revelation of child sexual abuse (Giaretto 1981). Whereas the child protectionist lobby had little direct concern for the adults in families where child sexual abuse had occurred, Giaretto saw families as the key area of focus. In his view, family dynamics helped create the conditions for child sexual abuse and the family was seen as the forum within which problems could (and should) be resolved. Giaretto developed his approach early in the 1970s. Essentially he aimed to support families where sexual abuse had occurred by providing help and treatment for the alleged abuser (as opposed to the more punitive and negative effects of incarceration), and by supporting other members of the family through individual and group therapies. This family perspective on child sexual abuse was particularly influential throughout the early period of child sexual abuse 'discovery', and indeed was shared to some degree by child protectionists (see Mrazek and Kempe 1981). The following quotes give some idea of the flavour of what has been termed the 'family dysfunction' approach to child sexual abuse:

Clinically incest appears to be part of an interpersonal triangle in which the collusion of the non-participating members is of primary importance. (Rist 1979, p.685)

The victim and the offender need to be counseled and treated with compassion and understanding. The offender is the family scapegoat, the member who acts out the problems of the entire family. Every family member must examine his or her responsibility and motivations regarding family functioning. Thus one must consider the problem of sexual abuse a family problem, treat the abuse as if it were another symptom of family stress in a maladaptive way and begin working on family roles and relationships. (Jorne 1979, p.289)

Offender-focused Approaches

A third influence came from psychologists and psychiatrists working with alleged and convicted child sexual abusers, both intrafamilial and, more frequently, extrafamilial. In sharp contrast to the previous perspective, the focus of these professionals was on the behaviour of abusers and on why they sexually abused children. For the most part, abusers were seen by these professionals as having serious personality problems and as being an ongoing danger to children without proper intervention. They were seen as unlikely to desist from sexual abuse without the intervention of the criminal justice system, and as amenable to treatment only in a small number of cases. Writers and practitioners such as Groth (Groth 1979; Groth and Birnbaum 1978) were at pains to point out that many abusers were likely to continue to abuse without intervention and that professionals involved in child protection work needed to be unequivocal about speedy intervention and separation of abuser and abused.

The Feminist Approach

The last of the influences, though by no means the least, was that of the feminist movement from the early 1970s onwards. L. Gordon (1989, p.4) argues that throughout recent history, 'Concern with family violence usually grew when feminism was strong and ebbed when feminism was weak. Women's movements have consistently been concerned with violence not only against women but also against children.' Feminism was strong in the USA in the 1970s. The assertion of equal occupation rights and the rejection of ascribed female roles were the main targets of the feminist movement, but alongside these developments came a re-examination of all aspects of the lives of women, including sexual relations and sex oppression. Women's experiences of male sexuality were seen by feminists in the USA as reflective of patriarchy, and the oppressiveness of these male–female relations was most clearly demonstrated by rape and the abuse of female children within the family. Thus what was previously thought best repressed and kept quiet became something to make public and political. Accounts of sexual abuse survivors such as Armstrong (1978) and Brady (1979) had considerable impact when they were published. Rush (1980), who had been campaigning on these issues throughout the 1970s, encapsulated the feminist perspective in clear and unequivocal language. For her, child sexual abuse was undoubtedly a direct effect of the oppression of women by men, institutionalized by patriarchy. From the feminist perspective, there was little difference between extra- and intrafamilial abuse except the setting and the tactics. Sexual abuse was a crime requiring legal intervention, punishment and, to a lesser extent, treatment. Not surprisingly, feminists were highly critical of family dysfunction approaches which related sexual abuse to family dynamics and, in their view, diverted attention (and blame) from offending males.

Common Ground

Whatever the particular perspectives held, by the start of the 1980s there was common agreement among child protection practitioners and writers on child sexual abuse in the USA on the following factors:

- that child sexual abuse in general was not, as previously thought by many, a rare occurrence. Heightened awareness on the part of professionals involved in child protection and child molester work contributed to this development. Another factor was the use of prevalence studies in the general population. The first of these, reported on by Finkelhor in 1979, indicated that 19 per cent of college women and 9 per cent of college men had been subjected to some form of sexual abuse, either intrafamilial or extrafamilial, before the age of 16 (Finkelhor 1979b)

- that intrafamilial sexual abuse was similarly not such a rarity as had previously been thought. Russell, writing in 1986, pointed to such abuse affecting 16 per cent of female children before the age of 18 and 12 per cent before the age of 14. Two-thirds of this abuse was categorized as severe or very severe

- that intrafamilial child sexual abuse was not limited to poor, ignorant and deprived families. There was general agreement that such abuse could take many forms (see Summit and Kryso 1978), and that children of all classes and backgrounds were vulnerable to it. This view was based on clinical experience and the findings of prevalence studies such as those of Finkelhor and Russell, just referred to, and it was made sense of by feminist views that the patriarchal nature of societies created the conditions for child sexual abuse to take place

- that the testimony of children was in most cases likely to be true. The tendency for professionals to use Freudian theory to explain children's allegations of abuse as wish fulfilments linked to their early psycho-sexual development was greatly diminished during this period. Psychoanalysts such as Miller (1985) were accepting children's stories as true rather than as fantasies

- that child sexual abuse potentially could have long-term health implications. Accounts of survivors pointed to debilitating effects, such as low self-esteem, lack of trust, depression, suicide and sexual difficulties in adulthood. It was generally agreed among professionals that such effects could not be tolerated and needed bringing into the open in order to be dealt with (see Browne and Finkelhor 1986). The old philosophy of 'turning a blind eye' or 'leaving well alone' was considered well and truly unacceptable.

The Modern-day Response – Britain

Pre-Cleveland

These ideas impacted on the British scene at the beginning of the 1980s (see Mrazek and Kempe 1981). The four perspectives on child sexual abuse outlined in the previous section were replicated in the approaches of child sexual abuse practitioners in Britain from this time onwards. This was no accident. British health and welfare work has traditionally sought ideas from, and been influenced by, the American scene.[1]

Child protectionists in Britain were not particularly vociferous at this time about the development of work in the area of child sexual abuse. There are few written accounts of how social workers and other professionals were functioning during this period. There were some contributions from social work educationalists (e.g. Christopherson 1981) and accounts were also written about paediatric-led interventions (e.g. Wild 1986). However, work being carried out by social workers in statutory and voluntary social services agencies went largely unrecorded and, therefore, there is little detailed information of how exactly child sexual abuse awareness and intervention strategies developed in this early period. From discussions with practitioners in the area in

---

[1] Baher et al. (1976) provide a detailed account of how the NSPCC transported the ideas of Kempe and his associates to Britain for dealing with physically abused and neglected children.

which this study was carried out, it seems that the key movers at this time in statutory settings were child protection/child care workers (mainly female) who were sensitized to sexual abuse by their own experiences (both personal and with female clients). Some of these workers were involved as volunteers in Rape Crisis work. Most were influenced by feminist perspectives. A combination of increased awareness of the problem (resulting in an increasing referral rate) and a commitment to develop forms of practice that were in line with the most recent thinking about dealing with child sexual abuse, led social workers such as these to adopt the ideas and techniques being pioneered in the USA. The most notable of these new practices were child-centred interviewing and the use of anatomically correct dolls.

The family dysfunction approach developed by Giaretto in the 1970s in the USA (Giaretto 1981) was to some degree replicated in Britain by the work of Arnon Bentovim and his colleagues at the Great Ormond Street Hospital from as early as 1981 (Bentovim *et al.* 1988). The similarities between the two approaches centred around seeing family dynamics as the key factors in the occurrence of intrafamilial child sexual abuse. In practice, workers at Great Ormond Street were not able to work with families as easily as Giaretto in California because of the differences between the two criminal justice systems. Whereas Giaretto had the facility to use a treatment programme as an alternative to prosecution, this was not available (and is still not available) in English law. Much of the work with offenders and their families carried out by Bentovim and his colleagues took place after conviction and the serving of a prison sentence. The Great Ormond Street team did, however, develop a wide range of other child sexual abuse work methods around disclosure and follow-up work with abused children and non-abusing parents. Feminists, however, have been particularly critical of their approach and that of other proponents of family dysfunction theory because, it is argued, it implies a shared responsibility for the occurrence of child sexual abuse rather than placing it firmly in the court of the (mainly male) abuser (Macleod and Saraga 1988).

The interest in work with offenders was promoted particularly by Wyre (1987) from the middle of the eighties. It has to be noted, however, that work of this kind was rare and directed mainly at serious or repetitive offenders, most of whom had been convicted of extrafamilial sexual abuse offences. The exception to this was the work of forensic psychologists who in some regions were developing both methods of helping children divulge abuse and of working with intrafamilial abusers.

Feminist approaches, though not concerted or coordinated, were being developed where there were strong pockets of such thinking – around Rape

Crisis Centres and some academic centres (usually in large cities). As pointed out above, much of the driving force behind child protectionists in Britain came from female practitioners with an awareness of feminist philosophy.

The speed with which child sexual abuse was taken up during this period is reflected in the statistics. NSPCC register returns, which until 1988 were used to give some estimate of the extent of officially detected child abuse, showed that between 1984 and 1988 the number of sexual abuse registrations had increased nearly six-fold from just over 1000 to nearly 6000 (Creighton 1992).

This fast-growing response to child sexual abuse, however, came almost solely from professionals who worked with children and from the pressure created by female abuse survivors. By contrast, the response of the state (in the form of central government guidance) was low key and *laissez-faire*. It was not until the Cleveland affair in 1987 that central government grasped the nettle of child sexual abuse and, even then, it was in a negative and defensive way. A good example of this limited response is the fact that sexual abuse was not made an official category for child protection registration until 1988 (though it was clearly stated as grounds for care proceedings in the 1969 Children and Young Persons Act).

The picture prior to Cleveland, therefore, was as follows. In some parts of the country there was considerable awareness of child sexual abuse, and in others there was very limited awareness. A great deal depended on personnel issues, that is, whether there were enough practitioners in an area who were sufficiently prepared and committed to tackling what was for many a difficult and unpalatable problem. This was certainly true in the medical and psychological fields. Thus centres of expertise developed, such as in Leeds and London, which other professionals in the region could refer to and learn from,[2] but those living in other areas did not have a similar facility. The situation was paralleled in the case of the police. In some areas (for instance, Bexley, Northumbria and North Yorkshire) police forces sensitized by criticisms of their handling of rape cases in the early 1980s, had developed specialist teams

---

2   The work of Bentovim, despite criticisms from those with a feminist perspective, was particularly influential in the London area and nationally in the development of techniques for investigating child sexual abuse allegations. In Leeds, the work of two paediatricians, Hobbs and Wynne, was instrumental in setting up a relatively advanced system for responding to child sexual abuse cases (see Butler-Sloss 1988, pp.220–221 and pp.313–319, Appendix L). Their work on the buggery of small children (Hobbs and Wynne 1986) was a direct influence on the work of Marietta Higgs and Geoffrey Wyatt in Cleveland.

to deal with child sexual abuse[3]. In other areas no special facilities had been created. Social workers, despite having a statutory remit to intervene to protect children thought to be in need of care and protection, did not develop a uniform response to the problem. Much depended on whether there were committed (usually female) individuals in an area. Most social services departments at this time were preoccupied with developing watertight systems for dealing with physical abuse and neglect of children in response to the criticisms levelled at them by various public inquiries.

Paradoxically, however, despite the geographical patchiness of the response to child sexual abuse, there was a growing degree of consistency among those child protection professionals who were committed to dealing with such abuse with regard to beliefs and practices. By 1987, these common factors were as follows:

1. There was agreement that investigations should be carried out within the framework of the then existing child protection procedures with their emphasis on a child-centred focus and multi-disciplinary practice.[4]

2. Child sexual abuse was seen as a serious crime requiring police intervention in most cases. It was not seen as a social/familial problem resolvable by social work intervention alone.

3. Social workers and health professionals adhered to some strongly held views, namely that children do not lie about sexual abuse and that all such abuse is likely to have long-term ill-effects without prompt protective intervention.

3   A TV documentary produced by Roger Graef on ITV in 1983 carried out a fly-on-the-wall observation of the practices of the Thames Valley police. One of the cases observed was that of a highly insensitive response by a male police officer to a rape allegation made by a young woman. Public reaction to the programme was one of considerable outrage and prompted a rethink of the way in which rape victims should be treated by investigating authorities. In the mid-1980s, the Metropolitan Police Force, in conjunction with Bexley social services department, carried out a piece of action research pioneering joint investigations of child abuse allegations (Metropolitan Police and London Borough of Bexley 1987) which acted as something of a blueprint for such investigations, and certainly after Cleveland. The Northumberland and North Yorkshire police forces are referred to as good examples of practice in the Cleveland Report (Butler-Sloss 1988, pp.223 and 224).

4   By 1986, the child protection system in England and Wales was characterized by three features: (1) Area Review Committees, which were interdisciplinary forums for middle and higher managers of police, health, welfare and education departments, and produced a manual of procedure to act as a guide to investigations; (2) interdisciplinary case conferences, which were held on each new case considered to be serious enough to warrant formal consultation; and (3) child abuse registers. The workings of the child protection system will form a major part of the following study, but for a more detailed overview see Corby (1995).

4. Certain techniques, such as child-centred interviewing using play activity as a means of gaining trust, were seen as key child sexual abuse intervention strategies by health and welfare professionals.

5. The immediate protection of children (using wardship or place-of-safety orders) was seen as essential in cases where the alleged abuser was likely to remain in the household. This view was influenced to some extent by the criticisms of lack of positive action in much-publicized physical abuse cases such as Jasmine Beckford (London Borough of Brent 1985) and Kimberley Carlile (London Borough of Greenwich 1987).

A picture emerges, therefore, of an increasingly consistent form of practice being developed among 'informed' professionals. In some areas these new ways of thinking were shared across professions. In other areas they were almost non-existent, and in yet other areas they were held by some professionals and not by others. Thus it was possible to have some areas with a very committed child sexual abuse network, others with a very limited one and others where there was disagreement and conflict about how to proceed. In the 'enlightened' areas, rates of official discovery of child sexual abuse were likely to be higher because of the greater awareness and vigilance that the new knowledge generated. Rates of registration were likely to be lower in the mixed areas and lower still where there was limited awareness of the issues. This state of affairs arose because no goals, priorities or requirements were being set by central government or by higher management within social services departments.

The Cleveland Crisis

Events in 1987 at Cleveland ensured government intervention and a more concerted effort to develop a top-led strategy in respect of child sexual abuse.[5]

5   In July 1987, it was reported that a hospital in Middlesborough was overflowing with children being kept on the wards there as a result of suspicions that they had been sexually abused. It emerged that 121 children has been made the subject of place-of-safety orders on these grounds over a period of 6 months, a rate of case confirmation which far exceeded that of other areas at this time and that of Cleveland itself prior to this period. A particular medical test, that of anal reflex dilatation, had been used to confirm all the suspected cases of abuse. While by the time the inquiry reported the vast majority had been returned to their family homes, the inquiry did not try to assess whether the children concerned had been abused. Instead it focused on the interventive practices regardless of this fact. Some of the practitioners at Cleveland are still convinced that the majority of the children they diagnosed as being sexually abused were abused (see Bacon and Richardson 1991). These issues were raised again most recently in a Channel 4 television documentary entitled 'Death of Children (Cleveland)', broadcast on 25 May 1997.

The Cleveland affair was the result of the process outlined above by which child protection policy in respect of sexual abuse was developed from the ground level up and not from the top down. In Cleveland there was a clash between professionals who were at different stages in thinking about child sexual abuse. The health and social work professionals were at the 'informed', heightened awareness end of the continuum, while the police and police surgeons were at the other end. The issue of gender may also have had an important influence – the leading health and social work protagonists were female and those from the police were male. This aspect of the situation was not raised in the Cleveland Report, but it is persuasively highlighted by Beatrix Campbell's analysis of events (Campbell 1988). The Cleveland Report (Butler- Sloss 1988) maintained a degree of neutrality between the progressives and the traditionalists by criticizing both sets of professionals equally, particularly for their failure to come to some form of compromise and work together. However, it was unequivocal in its condemnation of the way in which some of the new ideas and methods of intervention had been put into practice. The medical tests were seen as unreliable on their own; the interventive practices of social workers (which entailed a series of lengthy interview sessions with children to enable them to disclose abuse) were seen as oppressive; and there was criticism of the practice of automatically removing children suspected of being abused into emergency care.

The overall message that emerged from Cleveland was that there was a need for a more careful, controlled and coordinated approach to the issue of child sexual abuse. Contrary to what had been seen to be the case with physical child abuse and neglect, it was felt that intervention into sexual abuse cases could, unless carefully orchestrated and strategically planned, do more harm than good. While Lord Chief Justice Butler-Sloss, the author of the report, was keen to ensure that child sexual abuse remained an important item on the social policy agenda, the overall message was a clear vote of no confidence in many of the bottom-up developments of the previous half-decade.

What Cleveland specifically recommended was that there should be joint training for police and social workers for carrying out investigations, and that in future most investigations should be carried out jointly. It also recommended the need for more focused and less protracted interviewing of children, and the need to find alternatives to removing from home children suspected of being sexually abused unless absolutely necessary. It emphasized the need to consult with both children and parents about courses of action.

Although what happened at Cleveland and the publication of the ensuing report were key events in shaping child sexual abuse interventions in the late 1980s and early 1990s, other developments also contributed, two of which are particularly worthy of mention. First, new child care legislation had been in the offing since the findings of the Short Report in 1984 (House of Commons 1984), the final outcome of which was the 1989 Children Act. This legislation emphasized children's rights and parental responsibilities, reflecting some of the concerns raised in the Cleveland Report. Another important strand of development was work promoted by the Home Office with regard to the criminal law, the prosecution of sexual abuse offenders and the status of the evidence of children (see Cobley 1995).

Post-Cleveland

In the period after Cleveland, the following key developments in relation to the investigation and management of child sexual abuse allegations took place:

1. In 1988 'Working Together' guidelines published by the Department of Health and Social Security were circulated. The main features of these guidelines were, first, that sexual abuse should be a separate registration category; second, that parents (and children, where age appropriate) should be invited to attend child protection conferences, either in part or throughout;[6] third, that there should be joint interviews (by police and social workers) of children about whom there were serious child protection concerns; and fourth, that medical examinations should be subject to the child's consent where she/he was considered of sufficient age and understanding, and that they should be carried out jointly by child physicians and forensic doctors. With regard to police/social worker joint interviewing, a 1988 Home Office circular advised chief police officers to discuss joint training initiatives with directors of social services (Home Office 1988).

---

6   The contrast between the advice given in draft guidelines in 1986, which were issued in the wake of the Beckford inquiry (London Borough of Brent 1985), and the post-Cleveland 1988 guidelines demonstrates how sudden and dramatic a change took place. The following advice on parental attendance at child protection conferences is given in the 1986 guidelines: 'It is not appropriate for parents to attend the latter [formal inter-agency case conferences] which are professional meetings focused on the details of interagency co-operation to protect the child and plan for the future' (DHSS 1986, p.19).

     In 1988 the advice is: 'They [the parents] should be invited where practicable to attend part or if appropriate the whole of case conferences unless in the view of the Chairman of the conference their presence will preclude a full and proper consideration of the child's interests' (DHSS 1988, para. 5.45). For a fuller discussion of this issue see Parton (1991, pp.130–132).

2. The 1988 Criminal Justice Act made it possible for children to be cross-examined in court by video-link rather than have to face the accused directly. It also made changes to the corroboration rules, enabling a child's testimony to be legally acceptable without corroborating evidence (i.e. to have the same weight as that of an adult). However, trial judges were required to warn juries that it would be dangerous to convict on the evidence of the complainant alone! The need for such a warning was not finally removed until the passing of the 1994 Criminal Justice and Public Order Act.

3. In 1991 new Working Together guidelines were issued to accompany the implementation of the 1989 Children Act (Department of Health 1991a). These further emphasized the need to listen to children and involve parents. Local authorities were encouraged to find (and enabled to defray the expenses of) accommodation for alleged intrafamilial abusers. Police were also encouraged to use new powers under the 1991 Criminal Justice Act to impose bail conditions on alleged abusers to keep them away from their alleged victims. The intention of both these measures was, in the wake of Cleveland and later inquiries (see below), to protect abused children with the minimum possible disruption to their lives.

4. The 1991 Criminal Justice Act made it lawful to use investigative videos as evidence-in-chief in criminal trials of alleged child sex abusers. In 1992 the Memorandum of Good Practice was issued by the Home Office, detailing the conduct and content of such videos in order to meet the requirements of the courts (Home Office 1992). The main features of this Memorandum are the demands for high technical standards of videoing and stringent rules about acceptable forms of questioning and about the length and number of interviews. The Advisory Group on Video Evidence, chaired by Justice Pigot and set up by the Home Office (Home Office 1989), had recommended that ways be found to avoid full cross-examination of children in court about the evidence given on video. Their proposals were rejected on the grounds that they impinged too heavily on the rights of defendants.

The thrust of these developments was as much to limit the pre-Cleveland type of child sexual abuse investigation as to enhance it. Contrary to what had been expected in physical abuse cases, in sexual abuse cases, strict procedural action was seen to be more important than speedy and decisive intervention. This shift in approach was reinforced by concerns raised about social work interventions in the early 1990s into cases where organized or ritual abuse was suspected in Rochdale, Manchester, Nottingham and the Orkneys (see Lyon and DeCruz 1993, pp.54–57), the latter case resulting in another highly publicized statutory inquiry. The concerns in all these cases were not about a lack of inter-agency cooperation, as was true in Cleveland – ironically, police and social workers acted very much in conjunction. Rather, the issue was the precipitateness of the action taken by child protection professionals without properly informing parents of concerns and without due consideration of the needs and wishes of the children involved. In the Orkneys (Clyde 1992), where there were concerns that nine children from four different families were being subjected to a form of sexual abuse involving several adults and the local minister in night-time Satanic rituals, the police and social services department had planned their intervention very carefully. Children were removed from their homes in the early morning before they could leave for school (emergency orders having been sought the previous day – without the parents being consulted) and placed with foster parents on the mainland of Scotland that same day. They were each interviewed by social workers on many occasions (without video), and parents were refused access in person or by letter. Eventually the cases were dropped because of lack of evidence, and the actions of the authorities were severely criticized by Lord Clyde in his report.

The logic of the intervention of the child protection professionals was that ritual abuse could not be tackled by normal procedures, because the alleged abusers often held some supernatural hold over their victims which would lead the latter to retract their allegations if they continued to remain under their influence (and in contact with them). A similar sort of logic had prevailed in relation to intrafamilial abuse to a lesser degree in Cleveland. However, such thinking was rejected as being unacceptable by the Orkneys Report. There followed a Department of Health-sponsored survey which found that there was almost no concrete evidence of Satanic ritual abuse of children in Britain (LaFontaine 1994). However, a separate study (Gallagher, Hughes and Parker 1996) found considerable evidence of organized abuse (i.e. abuse involving either multiple abusers or victims or both).

In general there is still a great deal of public disquiet over the intervention methods used by child protection professionals (and social workers in particular) to investigate child sexual abuse. The Rochdale and Orkneys cases, because of their subject matter, that is, ritual abuse, seemed to confirm a view that the social work profession was obsessed with rooting out perversion and child abuse even if there was only the slightest of suspicions. The debate about the existence of ritual abuse goes on, despite the findings of LaFontaine's research (see Cook and Kelly 1997; Paley 1997). It seems impossible to get to the bottom of this particular issue, and, strategically, it is probably best for social workers to let the police play a leading role in this. However, there are dangers that the outcomes of the focus of concerns with ritual abuse (and public response to this) could impact negatively on the strength of response to intrafamilial sexual abuse cases and the type of organized abuse researched by Gallagher and his colleagues.

Summary

This, therefore, is the context in which the study which is the subject of this book took place. The field research spanned four years, from the last two months of 1989 to 1993. In 1989, the Cleveland recommendations, transmitted through the 1988 Working Together guidelines, were beginning to filter through into practice. During the research, the 1989 Children Act and two Criminal Justice Acts were implemented. In 1992, the procedure for carrying out joint interviews was changed significantly by the introduction of the Memorandum of Good Practice. Two key developments characterized this period of child protection development. The first was the shift from a front-line-led form of practice to a more top-led strategy. The second was a retrenchment from the previous child rescue approach to child sexual abuse to a more defensive position and philosophy. A key concern of the research is to examine what impact these changes had on child protection professionals (particularly social workers) and the way in which they carried out this work. The more detailed aims of the research and methodology used are outlined in the following chapter.

CHAPTER 3

Aims and Methodology

Broad Aims

As stated in the Introduction, the general aim of this book is, first, to examine how child sexual abuse is investigated and followed through by social workers and other child professionals. What originally prompted the research which forms the body of the book was the fact that the main documented examples of such child sexual abuse intervention available to the general public were the findings of public inquiries into cases where things had gone palpably wrong. While such cases undoubtedly provide sobering lessons and caveats for child protection professionals, they do not necessarily provide an accurate picture of the range of work that is encountered daily by social workers and others, or of the way in which they normally tackle these situations (see Hallett 1989). Events in Cleveland (Butler-Sloss 1988), for example, were atypical of the approach in many areas because of the degree of conflict between the professionals there and the intensity of the referral rate in the period leading up to the final crisis. The first general aim of this research, therefore, is to provide some data about child sexual abuse work in what could be perceived as more 'normal' or 'typical' conditions.

A second general aim is to examine how child sexual abuse work has been affected by the findings of the Cleveland Report and subsequent advice and guidance from central government. The research was begun at the end of 1989, just over a year after the publication of the Cleveland inquiry report. At this time the report seemed to be having two main impacts. First, most child protection workers were making efforts to avoid acting in the same way as the Cleveland professionals, and, second, Area Child Protection Committees were beginning to operate a tighter managerial control of front-line practice. During the research period (i.e. up to the end of 1993), many formal changes to policy and practice were made, as outlined in the previous chapter. The research was concerned to see how these changes influenced work on the ground.

Social Services Department Social Workers

The main focus of the research is on the way in which social services department social workers respond to the demands of child sexual abuse referrals and the ongoing work that might arise from their investigations. The focus is on these social workers, first, because they are pivotal personnel throughout the whole process of child abuse work. They have a key role in the referral/investigation process alongside the police. They have a lead role in gathering information for the assessment of cases for potential registration and for the need for continuing work with families, reporting to the child protection conference. They and (to a much lesser extent) NSPCC social workers, are the only professionals who can be appointed at child protection conferences to be key workers with responsibility for implementing and overseeing child protection plans. They have a statutory remit to initiate care proceedings and provide residential care and community supervision for children considered to be in need of such protection. Given this range of roles and responsibilities, research through such social workers gives access to a broad range of activities which is not achievable through other professionals who carry out more limited and prescribed roles within the child protection system.

A second reason for selecting social services department social workers as the main focus of research is a practical one. My own professional background as a social worker has enabled me to gain access to this professional group more easily.

Other Professionals

Despite the primacy of social services department social workers in child protection work, it is clear that such work also has a strong interprofessional element to it. Certainly, this is what is expected by central government, which, acting on the findings of numerous public inquiries over the past 20 years (see DHSS 1982; DoH 1991b), has strongly encouraged the development of an interdisciplinary approach via the establishment of Area Child Protection Committees and the publication of the various sets of circulars and guidelines (DHSS 1974a, 1980, 1988; DoH 1991a). While the extent and quality of interprofessional collaboration vary in different parts of the country (see Hallett and Birchall 1992), and it has been argued by many practitioners and commentators that much more could be done to improve the situation (see particularly Dale et al. 1986; Furniss 1991), an interdisciplinary approach is considered to be a key element in the protection of children. Therefore, although this research is focused on social work practice, it incorporates much about the work of other professionals involved in child protection work. It should be stressed, however, that information about interdisciplinary work is derived mostly, but not exclusively, from the perspective of social work practitioners.

Parents and Children

This research does not focus heavily on the 'consumer' perspective. This is because the main aim of this research is to look at the problems of dealing with child sexual abuse allegations from the professional (particularly social work) perspective. The reason for taking this approach is the need, given the amount of public concern aroused by Cleveland and the Orkneys, to examine in detail what makes sexual abuse work such a problematic area of activity for those investigating it.

This is not to deny the importance of the views of the children and parents involved at the receiving end. The Cleveland Report emphatically demonstrated the urgent need to take their perspectives into account and the consequences of failing to do so. The development of policy and practice in the field of child protection should ultimately rely on as wide a range of relevant views as possible, and the consumer perspective (that of parents and children) should play a major role in this. Material from another study carried out by myself and colleagues (see Corby and Millar 1997; Corby, Millar and Young 1996) is presented in Appendix 2 to provide some examples of the impact of sexual abuse investigations on a small number of service users. Reference will also be made to the extensive Department of Health research published over the last two years (particularly Cleaver and Freeman 1995; Farmer and Owen 1995; Sharland et al. 1996; Thoburn, Lewis and Shemmings 1995). These research projects, sponsored by the government in the wake of Cleveland and other inquiries, are heavily focused on the consumer perspective and, therefore, fill a major gap in our understanding of child protection work.[1]

---

1   Indeed these studies demonstrate a dramatic shift of attention in child protection research to the consumer perspective. Prior to the publication of the Department of Health-sponsored research, very little attention had been paid to the views of parents and children at the receiving end of child abuse investigations in Britain. The main exceptions in the case of parents were the studies of Brown (1986) and Corby (1987) and, more recently, Hooper (1992). The child's perspective was probably even more neglected, Roberts and Taylor's (1993) study being one of the very few exceptions. There is some concern that the Department of Health's emphasis on the consumer perspective in the wake of the reaction to events in Cleveland has shifted the balance too far. Parton, while welcoming a consumer perspective, has argued (1996) that this research runs the risk of ignoring the problems faced by practitioners in investigating child protection.

    The key aims of the research project which is the subject of this book, namely to examine the complexities and problems of practice for child protection professionals, though not originally conceived as a counterbalance to an overabundance of consumer studies (they did not exist at the time), may to some extent serve this function.

Specific Aims

The more specific aims of the research are to answer the following questions:

1. How do social workers theorize, think about and understand child sexual abuse and to what extent is this thinking shared by other professionals?

2. What constitutes sexual abuse as far as state intervention is concerned? What is the range of the work which is considered to be the responsibility of child protection systems?

3. How do social services departments respond to allegations of child sexual abuse? How are cases allocated? How is this influenced by organizational issues such as the use of specialist or generalist workers? What impact do interprofessional relationships and arrangements have on this stage of the work?

4. How are investigations carried out? How are decisions reached about strategies of intervention?

5. What are the main concerns of professionals in the investigation stage? How do they make their assessments? How are common goals achieved? What is the role (and impact) of the child protection conference in this process?

6. How are cases followed up? Who carries out the follow-up work? What are the concerns in these early stages?

7. What is the effect or outcome of intervention into child sexual abuse?

Some key themes in researching these specific aims are as follows:

1. The extent to which a more top-down management of child sexual abuse work is in operation, how it is functioning and how social workers are responding to it.

2. How social workers react to being involved in closer working relationships with the police (given the history of a lack of common understanding and cooperation in the past).

3. How social workers involve children and parents more fully in the work that they are doing.

4. How a wide range of factors influence child sexual abuse work, including those of gender, specialism, team organization, interprofessional relationships, organizational structures and resources.

In summary, the concern of the research is to gain information about the problems and difficulties experienced by social workers (and, to a lesser extent, other child protection professionals) in carrying out child sexual abuse investigations and follow-up work.

Details of the Research Project

Timing

The research was conducted between November 1989 and December 1993. As was pointed out in the previous chapter, the context in which child sexual abuse work was carried out altered a good deal over this time. The Cleveland Report recommendations were made in 1988, and by 1989 joint training of child protection professionals (particularly that of police and social workers for the purposes of joint interviewing) was being implemented across the country. In 1991 the Rochdale case was in the news and the same year saw the publication of the Orkneys Report. From 1988 government guidelines had encouraged parental participation at child protection conferences (DHSS 1988). The 1991 guidelines (DoH 1991a) added more weight to this, making it clear that there had to be good reasons for excluding parents (and older children) (DoH 1991a, paras 6.15–6.17). 1991 also saw the implementation of the 1989 Children Act, and 1992 the publication of the Memorandum of Good Practice (Home Office 1992).

Much of the research into the early intervention stages of child sexual abuse interventions took place between late 1989 and early 1992. In effect, therefore, the impact of the Children Act and the Memorandum of Good Practice was not directly felt by many of the practitioners who were interviewed and observed at work. In one area studied, for instance, wardship was still being used up to 1991, but this was the exception. At a general level, the style of the child sexual abuse work included in this study anticipated the changes to come, if not the detailed content. For instance, joint interviewing was accepted practice in all the areas researched, but video interviewing facilities of the standard required by the Memorandum of Good Practice were not readily available. Parental (and child) participation at child protection conferences was beginning to take place, but not to the extent achieved more widely after 1991. Most areas were adopting a policy of non-removal of children from their homes, even though they did not have the authority to defray alleged abusers' additional living expenses until after October 1991 (see Schedule 5.2 of the 1989 Children Act). Despite the more recent policy changes, therefore, the issues for practitioners have not, in my view, changed substantially since the early 1990s.

The Research Process

The core of the research comprises an in-depth consideration of 40 child sexual abuse allegations that were the subject of child protection conferences in three local authorities in the North West of England. The selection of cases was a fairly random one. They were all new allegations made to eight particular teams in the three local authorities studied. Child protection case records and statistics for each authority were later examined in order to gain a broader picture of the range of child sexual abuse work carried out and were also used to check the representativeness of the sample. All 40 conferences were observed.

Follow-up interviews with key social workers were held at intervals of six weeks and six months after the conference. Twenty-eight first interviews were successfully completed, and 25 second interviews. No interviews were held in 12 cases, either because the decision reached at the conference was to take no further action and/or because social workers had not been allocated to cases. Thirty-seven case files were traced and read two years after the initial child protection conference.

Additional material was gathered from group interviews with representatives from the eight social services department area teams whose work was the subject of the study.[2]

A series of interviews (15 in all) were held with groups of other child protection professionals working with the 8 area teams. These included:

- police officers (2)
- police surgeons (2)
- clinical medical officers (3)
- health visitors (2)
- social services department child protection managers (2)
- schoolteachers (2)
- education welfare officers (1)
- probation officers (1).

Interviews with social workers lasted between 45 and 90 minutes and were all audio-taped and later transcribed. They were semi-structured in nature and mainly focused on facts and opinions relating to the particular cases with which the social workers were dealing.

---

2   Group interviews were held with ten teams in all.

The aims of the first interviews were to find out from the social workers what they considered to be the key issues in the cases, the facts of what had happened during the investigation process, and their opinions about what had happened and why. They were also asked about their views of how the child protection conference had been managed, about the decisions reached and about what had happened since the conference. Social workers were encouraged to talk freely about the factors that they considered to be important. Much of the interviewing then focused on clarification of matters that were unclear to the researcher and on the reasons for action being taken in the way that it was. Where the facts of the case were still unclear at the end of the interview, these were checked using information in the case files.

The aim of the second interviews was to receive an up-date from the social workers about events since the previous research interview. This entailed the researcher recapping events and the social worker taking up the story from there. The research method was the same as for the first interview. The researcher let the social worker describe key events in his/her own terms and asked for clarification and reasonings as and when appropriate.

The content of the interviews was analysed and, together with data from the case files and material derived from attendance at the child protection conferences, a factual data base about the cases was collected. The views and opinions of the social workers about various aspects of the child protection system and child sexual abuse were also collated.

Presenting the Findings

Research of this kind produces a mass of data which cannot all be included in an account of it. If it were all included, it would make very hard reading and there is no guarantee that it would greatly enhance the reader's understanding of the research phenomenon. Inevitably, therefore, there is a fair degree of selectivity in the presentation of data, and to some extent the interests and views of the researcher will determine what is selected and what is not. However, it must be recognized that in researching issues of this kind, there is no hard proof to be found. The material is qualitative and, therefore, it is inevitable that there will be a great deal of selectivity in both the process of carrying out the research and its presentation. As a consequence, it is important that sufficient raw data are provided for readers to make their own judgements about whether the conclusions reached in this study have validity. An attempt has been made in the following chapters, therefore, to tread a fine line between swamping readers with data overload on the one hand and with the researcher's opinions and prejudices on the other.

In what follows, a variety of presentation methods are used to achieve the goal of clarifying how child sexual abuse interventions are carried out and the reasoning behind the methods used. Initially, factual data relating to the 40 cases will be presented. In the ensuing chapters, focus will be placed on three stages of intervention: investigation, setting up protection plans and implementing them over a six-month period. Data will be used from all the sources outlined above to achieve this. Case studies will be used extensively as exemplars. These are of considerable importance because it is often the combination of circumstances and factors in particular cases that determines modes and styles of intervention. The complexity and interplay of such factors cannot be readily captured by statistical or other forms of analysis. Finally, the focus will be on what interventions seemed to achieve and what lessons can be learned from this sort of research.

CHAPTER 4

Setting the Scene

The Three Authorities

Research data were collected from three authorities in the North West region of England. The first, which will be termed City, is a large metropolitan area with many socio-economic problems, including high levels of poverty and un-employment. Between 1989 and 1993 (the period of the research), City authority had a child protection registration rate of between 6.2 and 8.1 per 1000 children under 18, over double the national average. The second authority, Seacoast, spreads from the border of City along the coast to a large seaside town. It has more of a socio-economic mix than City and includes some areas of urban deprivation and large expanses of middle-class suburbia. Between 1989 and 1993 the child protection registration rate varied between 2.2 and 3.6 per 1000, just below the national average. The third authority, County, is geographically very extensive, incorporating several industrial towns and a large rural area. Like Seacoast, the socio-economic picture is a varied one, with fairly high levels of deprivation in some of the industrial towns but considerable affluence elsewhere. Its registration rate varied between 1.8 and 2.4 per 1000 between 1989 and 1993, just under half the national average.

Eight area offices were selected as the focus of the research, four in City and two in each of Seacoast and County. The four areas of City included one central district where the levels of deprivation were very high and three offices on the periphery. In Seacoast, one of the two area offices selected bordered on City and there was little difference between it and the three offices at the edge of City. The second office covered a more socio-economically mixed area. The two offices in County were in industrial towns.

Sexual Abuse Statistics
The National Picture

Table 4.1 Children on child protection registers for child sexual abuse alone in England, 1989–93

Year	No. on registers	% of total on registers	Rates per 10,000 children
1989	5800	14	5.3
1990	5900	14	5.5
1991	5300	12	5.0
1992	5600	15	5.0
1993	7100	21	6.0

Source: Children and young persons on child protection registers year ending 31 March 1989, 1990, 1991, 1992 and 1993 (Department of Health).

Table 4.2 Annual registration numbers for child sexual abuse alone in England, 1989–93

Year	No. of registrations	% of total registrations	Rates per 10,000 children
1989	3800	17	3.5
1990	3800	14	3.5
1991	3400	12	3.0
1992	3800	15	3.0
1993	5600	22	5.0

Source: Children and young persons on child protection registers year ending 31 March 1989, 1990, 1991, 1992 and 1993 (Department of Health).

The picture provided nationally by the statistics shown in Tables 4.1 and 4.2 is that the number of children on registers and the number registered annually, for sexual abuse alone, remained constant for four years and then increased substantially. Figures for 1994 and 1995 show that this increase has been maintained.[1] This increase in sexual abuse registrations may be explained to some extent by a crucial change in the categorization of child abuse which took place in 1991 when 'grave professional concern', which had previously incorporated a large number of mixed categories of cases, was no longer used. From 1991, cases where there was concern that sexual abuse might have happened or was likely to happen in the future were more likely than before to be categorized under the heading of 'child sexual abuse'. This may account for the rise noted in the statistics rather than a real increase in the rate of detected sexual abuse. What is clear, however, is that these figures demonstrate that events at Cleveland, and later at Rochdale and the Orkneys, did not seem to discourage those professionals who were committed to working in this field from pursuing child sexual abuse with at least the same vigour as before, despite the formal criticisms of these cases in inquiry reports and court hearings, and the accompanying adverse publicity.

The Local Picture: Differences and Similarities

In the areas studied a varied picture emerges. Between 1989 and 1993, City had on average 85 children on its child protection register under the category of child sexual abuse. In 1989 it had 7 children per 10,000 on the register for sexual abuse and, in 1993, 11. Seacoast had on average 28 children registered for sexual abuse between these dates (2 per 10,000 in 1989 and 7 per 10,000 in 1993). County had an average of 44 registered (2 per 10,000 in 1989 and 1 per 10,000 in 1993). Thus, City was well above the national average, Seacoast was in line with the national average and County well below it. Numbers of registrations for sexual abuse per annum trebled in City between 1989 and 1993, increased by 50 per cent in Seacoast and were halved in County. In City, therefore, the registration rate increased well in excess of the national average. In Seacoast it rose in line with the national average and in County the trend was

---

1   The figures for 1994 and 1995 are as follows:

Number of children on registers for child sexual abuse

1994	8100 (23% of the total, representing 7 per 10,000 children)
1995	7500 (21% of the total, representing 7 per 10,000 children)

Number of children registered during the year for child sexual abuse

1994	6400 (22% of the total, representing 6 per 10,000 children)
1995	6000 (20% of the total, representing 5 per 10,000 children)

Source: Children and young persons on child protection registers year ending 31 March 1994 and 1995 (Department of Health).

in the opposite direction to that of the country as a whole.[2]

These figures could be taken to suggest that the rates of actual child sexual abuse in these three areas were very different. However, one needs to be cautious in drawing conclusions from child protection registration statistics – it has to be remembered that they refer only to those cases which have come right through the child protection system. Gibbons, Conroy and Bell (1995) found in their research that only 24 per cent of nearly 2000 child protection referrals resulted in case conferences being held and that only 15 per cent resulted in registration. They also found that there were considerable variations in registration rates in different authorities, suggesting differing interpretations of risk to children. Turning specifically to sexual abuse, Sharland et al. (1996) examined 147 referred cases of child sexual abuse and found that '2/3 of all cases and children referred to professional agencies for sexual abuse were filtered out of the child protection system before reaching the stage of conferencing or potential registration' (p.47). Indeed, by 12 months after referral for sexual abuse, only 11 per cent of children had been registered in this study. It would seem, therefore, that great care should be taken in interpreting statistics. Child protection registrations denote those cases that create sufficient concern to prompt professionals to ensure further ongoing work with the families involved. Therefore, it is likely that different registration practices in the three areas account to some extent for the statistical variation in officially known cases.

Information about all child sexual abuse referrals to these three areas was not available for the research that is the subject of this book. Thus it was not possible to examine which cases were filtered out of the system before the conference stage and, therefore, how and to what extent the practices of the different offices at this stage of the intervention process were at variance. It was possible to gauge practice at the conference stage, and the impression gained was that the following features of cases caused most concern in all three authorities: intrafamilial abuse, or the likelihood of such abuse (e.g. where there was a known schedule 1 offender living in the same household as children); where the alleged abusing relative or parent remained in the family; and where the non-abusing parent was thought to be a poor protector. Sharland et al. (1996) and Waterhouse and Carnie (1992) found similarly in their studies. Another factor which seemed to increase concern was a history of previous

2   It should be stressed that these figures are taken from County and Seacoast as a whole and that the specific areas selected for study included some of the most deprived areas of each of these authorities. Thus, though the figures for the whole authorities vary considerably, the differences between the actual districts studied were not as great as this suggests.

child protection involvement with families. In City and Seacoast, most of the cases of the kind outlined above tended to be registered. In County, while there was no less concern expressed about such cases than in the other two authorities, there was less readiness to register unless such registration was considered likely to have an impact in reducing risk.

It should be noted that a key factor common to all the authorities was the correlation between indices of social deprivation and child protection registration rates (including child sexual abuse registration). As has been noted above, City's rates of registration were overall higher than those of Seacoast and much higher than those of County, reflecting the indices of socio-economic deprivation in each of these areas. There has been much debate as to whether this correlation of deprivation and child protection registration reflects higher levels of abuse of children among the poorer classes or not – child protectionists, mainly committed to psychological explanations of child abuse, have tended to argue that child abuse is a cross-class phenomenon (see Kempe *et al.* 1962), and that the statistics are explained by the fact that the poor are more subject to state surveillance than wealthier families and so child abuse is much more likely to be spotted. In other words, the incidence of child abuse is not linked to poverty, but its discovery is (see Milner 1994). Those operating from a sociological perspective, who see child abuse as much more a product of living in stressful social conditions, argue that the statistics reflect the reality, namely that children living in poor families are more at risk of ill-treatment than their more privileged peers (Pelton 1978). In the case of sexual abuse, the argument for its cross-class nature has been made both by child protectionists using survey data (Finkelhor and Baron 1986) and feminists whose view is that sexual abuse is explained by gender and male power, not by class, poverty and ignorance (Macleod and Saraga 1988). As will be shown in the next chapter, most of the families which were the subject of this research were from the poorer sections of society and had experienced considerable deprivation. A smaller number of families in the sample were of the kind that would not normally have had contact with social services departments had the issue of sexual abuse not arisen.

It should be stressed, however, that despite variation in registration practices reflecting different philosophies about case management strategies between the authorities, and despite general differences in the socio-economic backgrounds of their populations, there were more common factors about the child sexual abuse interventions which were the subject of this research than distinguishing ones.

Organizational Arrangements for Responding to Child Sexual Abuse

In the following sections of this chapter the focus is placed on the way in which the three authorities organized their child sexual abuse work. Information about the organizational response was taken from group interviews with social work teams and other child protection professionals' groups. Additional information was gained from discussions with child protection coordinators and from documentary sources provided by the social services departments concerned.

The Formal Response to Cleveland

All three authorities had responded to the guidance that followed the publication of the Cleveland Report (DHSS 1988). Much of the policy and practice in this document had been implemented in City, Seacoast and County by the end of 1989 when this study commenced. The main features of child sexual abuse investigations at this time were as follows:

1. Pre-investigation consultations between police and social services personnel for all allegations of child sexual abuse.

2. Joint interviewing by police and social services personnel of children alleging sexual abuse.

3. Joint medicals by police surgeons and hospital (or clinic) doctors for children alleging sexual abuse.

4. Child protection conferences for all sexual abuse cases where there was considered to be continued risk to children.

Specialization

County had a greater element of specialism than either Seacoast or City. One of the teams studied specialized solely in child protection investigation work. In the other team, two specialist child protection workers were attached to the intake/short-term assessment team. They had an advisory/training role for their agency's social workers and for other professionals involved in child protection work. They also took responsibility for some of the more problematic child protection investigations (including particularly those involving child sexual abuse allegations).

In Seacoast and City, the responsibility for child protection investigations fell to intake or short-term assessment teams. These teams were theoretically generic, but in practice much of their time was taken up with child protection investigations. In Seacoast, individuals who wished to develop their expertise in child sexual abuse work were encouraged to do so by attendance on courses.

These social workers took a lead role in sexual abuse investigations, particularly with regard to interviewing children, but other social workers in the teams were expected to carry out child sexual abuse investigations as well. The City teams which were studied neither employed specialists nor particularly encouraged informal specialisms. Child sexual abuse referrals were shared out equally among all the social workers. The only variable to have any influence other than availability was that of gender (see below).

In all areas, the intake/short-term assessment teams retained cases throughout the investigation period and often for appreciable periods afterwards, usually because of difficulties in transferring cases to hard-pressed long-term teams. On average, active cases were held for six months (or longer if court proceedings were taking place) before such referrals took place.

Training

In all three authorities, the majority of social workers dealing with child sexual abuse investigations had received some form of in-service training for child protection work. Most said that their qualifying training had placed very little emphasis on child sexual abuse – this was particularly true of those who had qualified before 1985. A high percentage of County social workers had completed joint training with the police, as had a smaller number of Seacoast's social workers. None of City's social workers had been involved in such training. Similarly, more of County and Seacoast's social workers had attended short specialist training programmes on topics such as raising sexual abuse awareness and child interviewing. One social worker in each of these authorities had completed longer-term post-qualifying courses in child protection. Again, far fewer of City's social workers had attended short courses and none had been involved in more extensive training programmes.

In general terms, the level of training and knowledge was low. Fisher (1997) reports a similarly low level of training for child protection social workers who were the subject of a research project in 1994.

Dealing with New Referrals

All but one of the teams studied had a system of duty whereby intake/short-term assessment team workers took referrals and either followed them up themselves or passed them on to other team members if available. The exception was in the County district, where there was a specialist child protection team. This district employed two full-time duty workers who went out on initial investigations if none of the specialist workers were free to do so. In none of the areas, therefore, was investigative work necessarily carried out by specialist workers or by those with the most expertise in child sexual abuse work. Case allocation was generally determined by availability rather than by worker expertise. This was particularly the case in City, where many of the intake team social workers were relatively inexperienced. In all areas, social workers carried out initial investigations in pairs unless it was decided that the first contact should be in the form of a joint interview with the police.

The investigative procedures were similar in all areas. New referrals were discussed with team leaders. Checks with other agencies and child protection registers were standard practice. Team leaders were responsible for liaising with the police to decide on courses of action. In all three authorities there was a protocol for liaison, but in most areas such liaison was still seen as problematic. Much depended on the development of good relationships between individuals in the two agencies. As has been seen, social workers were not organized in a specialist way. The police were more specialized in their approach than the social workers, but in some areas there was only one specialist police worker and frequently she/he was not available for liaison or for carrying out joint interviews. Only in one of the County teams was police/social services department liaison relatively smooth. In this area a police child protection team was housed in the same set of offices as the social services department workers and a close working relationship had developed, particularly since the outcome of the Cleveland affair.

Joint Interviews

In most of the areas there was confusion about when and when not to do joint interviews. Despite efforts to improve liaison between police and social services workers, and despite joint training, there was still a good deal of conflict between social workers and police on agreed courses of action. In some areas – Seacoast and one of the County teams in particular – social workers felt that the police were not interested if they felt there was little likelihood of a prosecution. One social worker who had recently attended a joint training course with the police described their approach as follows: 'We want a cough is the statement that remained right throughout the training. If we don't get it the inspector will be on our backs.' Social workers in these areas felt that the police were not, therefore, enthusiastic about following up cases of abuse of younger children (unless it was *prima facie* very serious) or cases where children were considered to be too vague about what had happened, because in both cases they were seen as unlikely to be able to give convincing testimony in court. Social workers in all areas (with the exception of one team in County) felt that more should be done to stay involved with such cases and to push harder for better evidence. They were of course able to do this themselves, but there was discouragement from such courses of action in the recommendations of inquiries such as Cleveland and the Orkneys, and the trend soon to be recommended in the Memorandum of Good Practice was against such an approach. It was notable that series of interviews were pursued by the Seacoast area teams, but County in particular, and City to a lesser extent, rarely carried out more than two investigative interviews.[3]

Joint interviews were held when there were clear allegations of abuse by children. In most cases where there was suspicion based on a child's behaviour or concern because of the presence in the household of a schedule 1 offender, such interviews were not common. At the time of the research, specialist interviewing suites with video facilities were in short supply. City social workers had the use of such facilities at a regional children's hospital. In County, NSPCC interviewing suites were available, but their use involved a good deal of travelling. Seacoast social services department developed its own facilities during the period of the research.

Most of the joint interviewing in this study took place, therefore, in social services department interviewing rooms or at children's centres. Use of video was rare. Efforts were made to ensure that interviewing took place in neutral non-threatening surroundings, and non-abusing parents and relatives were enabled to be present (particularly in the case of younger children). By and large, however, social workers were critical of the lack of, as they saw it, adequate facilities to conduct proper investigative interviews. As for the conduct of joint interviews, it was clearly felt that the police tended to dominate them and that the social workers played a secondary role. This was particularly true of City. A typical comment was as follows: 'We went to the Clinic where the child was being interviewed, but you couldn't say it was a joint interview. She [the police officer] did the work and I was in the room. She was more or less doing the interview.' The main focus of the interviews was to ascertain whether there was sufficient evidence for a prosecution of the alleged offender – hence the lead role taken by the police. The social worker's role was seen to be one of ensuring that the child was supported and comfortable in the process. Some social workers resented what they saw as a shift from the more child-centred approach that existed pre-Cleveland.

---

3   To some extent this may be explained by the fact that the Seacoast teams were focused on in the early part of the research project, that is, late 1989 and 1990. However, the tendency to stay involved longer in suspected cases remained a feature of the work carried out in Seacoast compared with City and especially County.

Medical Examinations

The procedure manuals in all three authorities formally required medical examinations for all children where there was an allegation of abuse. All areas had policies for ensuring that children should not be exposed to more than one examination and that there were arrangements for joint action by hospital/ clinic doctors and police surgeons. In fact a fair amount of discretion operated with regard to whether or not medical examinations would be required. Again, in the eyes of the social workers, the police had most say as to whether or not they should take place. Much seemed to depend on whether they thought that medical evidence would be needed to aid a conviction. In such cases they were insistent on the involvement of a police surgeon. There was uncertainty in general about the benefits of requiring medical examinations at all. Some social workers took the view that they were necessary in most cases because children might not have revealed the full facts about their abuse in the investigative interview. Others took the view that where allegations were not *prima facie* likely to result in any physical evidence, they were unnecessary.

In City, medical examinations and joint interviews could be carried out in the same suite at the regional children's hospital. Seacoast had some access to these facilities as well. County made more use of health centres for such examinations.

Child Protection Conferences

CHAIRING

Arrangements for conferences were different in each of the authorities. Seacoast operated a system whereby the area managers of each district chaired conferences. County had a child protection coordinator in each area who chaired conferences. City had a headquarters-based team of child protection coordinators, each responsible for chairing conferences at two or more district centres. Social workers in County felt supported by, and confident in, the conference system. They had easy access to conference chairpersons who were child protection specialists and this frequently meant that conferences held few surprises. As one social worker put it: 'The conference is confirming what has already taken place and just boxing issues off. It's more of a formal exercise really.' Similarly, in Seacoast the social workers had easy access to the conference chairpersons, but in this case they were not child protection specialists. In one of the areas studied there was considerable distrust of the chairperson/area manager, who was seen as unpredictable. In the other area, the opposite was true. In City, because the chairpersons were not area-based, there tended to be less prior consultation and more uncertainty about outcomes. In all areas studied, the impact of the chairperson was considerable in outcomes. In all areas studied, the impact of the chairperson was considerable in terms of the conduct of the conference and the clarity of decision-making (see Lewis 1994). In three areas studied, confidence was high, in four areas it was mixed and in one, already referred to, it was low.

PARENTAL PARTICIPATION

Despite the recommendations of the 1988 and 1991 Working Together guidelines (DHSS 1988; DoH 1991a), which reversed the previous policy of not including parents at conferences, there was little enthusiasm for parental participation and little progress in the areas studied until the later part of the research. County, surprisingly because in many other aspects it seemed to be the most closely tuned to governmental post-Cleveland organizational re-commendations, had the least participative policy. Parents were not allowed to attend any conferences (either initial or review) throughout the period of the research. Seacoast initiated a policy of parental participation during the course of the research. It had previously invited parents to meet with chairpersons of conferences and their social workers at the end of conferences in order to inform them of outcomes and seek their views about these. Its new policy encouraged parental attendance throughout initial conferences and reviews. City had a policy of partial attendance at initial conferences.

As will be seen, however, in the main body of the research findings, there was in fact very limited attendance of parents at the conferences that were the subject of this study. Social workers did not have strong feelings about the participation of parents. Some thought that the presence of parents would limit the amount of loose talk and opinion by professionals and thereby increase the objectivity of the decision-making process. Others felt that parents would find it very hard to cope with the conference situation.

Specialist Resources

At the time of the study there were few specialist resources for dealing with child sexual abuse in the areas examined. The police were the only agency which had developed a specialist response service. In County each police station had its own specialist child protection team. In City and Seacoast there were individual specialist police officers dealing with child protection. As has already been seen, there were two specialist workers in one of the County social services department teams and individuals who informally specialized in both County and Seacoast. The health services were not specialized with the exception of health visiting, which in each of the areas studied employed a nursing manager as a child protection liaison worker.

The NSPCC played a limited role in all the areas studied. NSPCC officers attended few conferences and carried out very few child protection investigations. They were in the process of developing post-investigative services in City.

There were very few other agencies that specialized in either investigative or therapeutic work. In City the regional children's hospital had recently developed a centre suitable for interviewing and carrying out medical examinations for evidence. The paediatricians there played an important role in ensuring a smooth investigative process. This facility was open to City and Seacoast. The former tended to make more use of it than the latter, largely because of geographical proximity, but at the time of the study the centre was not frequently used, possibly because of its newness but possibly also because fewer cases were seen as needing medicals and, therefore, referral to hospital. One of the County teams had no paediatric services directly available.

In City there was a forensic psychological service run by the health authority. This had played a pioneering role in the mid-1980s in developing therapeutic interviewing of children. By the end of the decade, however, it had shifted its focus more towards treatment of offenders. However, some use was still made of this service by all the authorities studied. The City magistrates were keen to have problematic assessments carried out by psychologists rather than by social workers, and there was growing concern about the need to assess and treat adolescent sex abusers. Another central resource based in City was a family therapy team run by a voluntary agency that took on cases referred by City, Seacoast and County, but particularly City and Seacoast. The regional hospital referred to above also provided some family-based therapy and some child-centred play therapy. However, all these services had small numbers of practitioners and, therefore, often had long waiting lists and limited capacity for taking on referrals. As will be seen from this study, little use was made of specialist resources for these and a variety of other reasons.

In all three authorities, social services department social workers ran groups for children who had been abused, and for adults who had either been abused themselves or whose children had been abused by their partners or both. Again, it has to be stressed that these groups did not provide a universal service. Access to them was frequently not available, and social workers and others who ran them often did so in their own time. There was provision in all areas for work with adult abusers by probation officers, but only if they had been convicted of offences.

Little use was made of family centre facilities in these three areas at the time of the study. In some areas they were available but not used and in others they were not available. It is not clear why they were not used more where they attached. Day nursery provision was more readily used where children were of the appropriate age.

Interprofessional Arrangements

Formally Area Child Protection Committees, known as Joint Child Protection Committees at the commencement of the study, managed arrangements for interprofessional cooperation over child protection issues in each of the areas studied. In the two County areas there were separate committees for each area as well as a county-wide committee. Seacoast and City each had one committee only. It was not possible to determine fully the extent to which these committees influenced child protection practice and interprofessional cooperation. However, each area committee had produced procedural manuals that were specific about investigation procedures for physical and sexual abuse allegations, spelling out the degree and type of cooperation expected. These committees were also responsible for interdisciplinary training (but not for all child protection training, which remained the responsibility of individual departments as part of their overall training strategies), and for monitoring the management of problematic cases.

COUNTY

The County teams seemed to have good interprofessional arrangements. There seemed to be considerable contact between agencies in these areas, and at conferences there was a good deal of familiarity between different professionals. In one of the County areas the interprofessional relationships seemed exceptionally good. There was close liaison between police and social services department social workers, who had offices very near to each other. There was a specialist police team. The sergeant in charge of this team met weekly with the child protection coordinator from the social services department and discussed newly referred cases. The police were generally happy with the response of social workers to child sexual abuse investigations and they felt that they understood and took into account their roles and responsibilities. There were occasional hiccups at case conferences where it was felt the child protection coordinators and social workers had already set their minds on courses of action and were not open to other agencies' concerns. There was some concern from the police about the possibility of parents being allowed to attend protection conferences; this was being discussed at the time of the research. Nevertheless, the general feeling of the police was that social workers were realistic and accepted the constraints under which they were operating. This view was reflected by the social workers in this area, who did not give the impression of being as powerless in relation to the police as most operating. This view was reflected by the social workers in this area, who did not give the impression of being as powerless in relation to the police as most of the other teams. This is exemplified by the following comment: 'This team would actually prevail on the CID and have done when they are raring to get out straight away.' There was a stronger feeling of equality between police and social workers here than elsewhere. Relationships with schools were also generally good. The two specialist child protection workers in the social services department were active in training teachers with a view to encouraging them to be more ready to make referrals. On the health side, a health visitor manager attended all conferences and there was good liaison with the clinic doctors (who had a key role to play because of the absence of paediatric medical support in the immediate area). There was some feeling among health personnel (as with the police) that social services workers tended to dominate, particularly in conferences. All in all, however, the interprofessional arrangements in this area were of a very high standard and a far cry from the situation in Cleveland. They were aided by the geographical proximity of the various departments and by the frequent contact between staff at the supervisor/middle-management level, particularly at conferences but in consultations prior to them as well.

The conditions for good interprofessional liaison were similar in the second County team, but lower levels of satisfaction were expressed by both social workers and other professionals. At the time of the research, social services department personnel resources were very stretched and this resulted in service users being unvisited for long periods, much to the annoyance of other departments – particularly the probation service and the health agencies. The child protection coordinator in this area had fostered good relationships with other agencies but this did not always filter down to the social services department social workers. In particular, there was not the same degree of trust between the social workers and the police in this area as there was in the other County area. This quote from a social worker should be compared with the one in the earlier paragraph: 'In practice it really depends on the attitude of the police and if the police think there's a job in it, the fact is that we move on it. If the police don't think there's a job in it, then that has a direct bearing on the response of this department as to what we do and how quickly we do it.' There is a sense of complete subservience to the requirements of the police force in this statement.

SEACOAST AND CITY

In Seacoast and City, interprofessional liaison was much more variable. In neither authority was much work done in a proactive way to enhance good working relationships. Also, neither had such good geographical advantages as in County. Boundaries of the various agencies were less coterminous, which led to the need to liaise with more sites. Thus most of the teams in these authorities had to liaise with two police stations and more than one health clinic. Consequently, there was a sense whereby good and bad contacts were seen more as the result of the luck of the draw than anything else. In these two authorities the prevailing view was that there were good and not so good individuals in different agencies. Good relationships were developed with particular individuals within agencies rather than between the agencies as a whole. This seemed to be particularly the case with the police. There was considerable praise for individual police officers, accompanied by fear of the fact that they might not be on duty when there was need for liaison. This view persisted in City despite middle-management negotiations to establish agreed protocols.

Part of the problem of cooperation was simply due to the size and diversity of agencies in City. In both City and Seacoast, child protection conferences and joint interviewing provided the main opportunities for developing inter-professional links, both of which can be fraught situations. Bad experiences in these situations can colour later experiences and lead to stereotyping (Hallett and Stevenson 1980). In Seacoast, as pointed out earlier, conferences in one of the districts were much better chaired (according to professionals' accounts) than in the other. This had more negative impact than it might have had if there had been other avenues for improving liaison. There were good contacts between health visitors and social workers in both authorities, but particularly in Seacoast, where it was policy for social workers and health visitors to carry out joint visits on physical abuse and neglect referrals. In one of the Seacoast areas there was criticism of social services department social workers by other involved professionals of the kind levelled at social workers in Cleveland: that there was a tendency to overreact and that they took on work for which they were not properly qualified, such as therapeutic investigations.

On the face of it, therefore, interprofessional liaison and communication was better in County than in the two other authorities. Seacoast seemed to be a little better in this respect than City. As pointed out above, the size and complexity of the different organizations was an important factor in deter-mining smooth inter-agency coordination. However, it should be stressed that there is little evidence to prove that good inter-agency cooperation is nec-essarily effective in tackling child abuse (see Hallett and Birchall 1992), and, as will be seen, there is nothing to suggest in this study that any one agency or team was more effective than others. Nevertheless, if, as has been suggested by Farmer and Owen (1995), a key impact of better interprofessional cooperation is to make professionals feel more secure about the work they are doing, this is clearly a benefit given the stressful nature of intervention into child sexual abuse situations. What is clear, however, is that in varying ways the lessons of Cleveland were being taken on board by all the agencies studied. There was no suggestion of the degree of rift which developed there.[4]

A Note on Gender

It was clear that issues of gender influenced policies and practice in all the areas studied. Gender was seen as important with regard to case allocation in social services departments. As far as possible, female social workers were allocated to children who had been abused by males, particularly in the case of girls. Male social workers were seen as appropriate workers with boys who had been abused, though there were some reservations about this on the grounds that the alleged abusers were invariably male. Male social workers were also seen as appropriate workers with young male abusers. Most social workers felt that children's and non-abusing parents' wishes should be the deciding factor in decisions about the gender of the worker. Only a few took the view that in no circumstances should male workers be involved in this work.[5] In some areas this was not an issue because there were only small numbers of male workers in the intake teams. In other areas, cases were allocated to whomever was available, and only if it was obviously inappropriate would male social workers be excluded. There were exceptions. In one of the Seacoast teams a male social worker was the key sexual abuse investigator, particularly with regard to the interviewing of young children.

4   A postal survey of social services departments' and police agencies' arrangements for carrying out child sexual abuse investigations in 1990–91 paints a very similar picture to that depicted here (see Moran-Ellis and Fielding 1996). The key points raised in this study were as follows: (1) joint approaches were well established but varied in type, depending particularly on geographical differences; (2) the police were much more likely to have developed specialist teams/workers; (3) training was patchy; and (4) joint interviewing facilities were variable in quality. The overall conclusion was that 'While the great majority of agencies identified themselves as working jointly, the variations in practice revealed by the survey require further scrutiny. There is need for continuing study of practice in relation to the investigation of child sexual abuse, particularly in the light of the tendency for innovations to lose their priority as other problems come to public notice' (p.355).

5   Pringle (1995) has put forward the view that serious consideration needs to be given to excluding males from this type of work because of the potential risk they present to children based on our knowledge of the predominance of male abusers. 'In such situations, the risk to the child's safety may be so great that we need to consider the possibility of restricting the access of men to work in those settings ... work with very young children in nursery care and day care; working with children with severe disabilities or with severe learning difficulties; work that focuses specifically on children and young people who have been sexually abused' (p.189). See also Frosh (1988).

As regards other agencies, wherever possible the police ensured that interviewers of young and female children were female. Efforts were made to ensure that there were sufficient female doctors on police surgeon lists, clearly reflecting an awareness of the need for female doctors to carry out medical examinations on female children.

Overall, therefore, in practice gender awareness was evident and influential where choice was possible. In terms of theorizing about the causes of abuse, some female workers, most particularly in City, supported the notion of patriarchal relations and the power differences between men and women as being important aetiological factors, but this line of thinking was not pursued heavily. Surprisingly, some female workers were strong in their condemnation of mothers who, as they saw it, failed to protect their children. There was a feeling among some workers that gender explanations were acceptable at the theory level, but they did not always relate them to practice. The following quotes from a discussion with social workers (all female) about whether service users in child sexual abuse cases preferred female social workers or not give some idea of the diversity of views:

SW 1 'I don't think people who are in crisis situations consider gender issues.'

SW 2 'I disagree – I think they do.'

SW 1 'Possibly girls do, but the boys I have interviewed have never once said, "I want a fellow".'

SW 3 'I think we have to act on the needs and stated preferences of the child.'

SW 2 'I think there is an assumption that if the victim is a female then you send out female workers. That is where we start. If there wasn't a female available then I think we would wait until the morning as long as it was safe.'

SW 1 'If they had a male social worker already it would be different.'

SW 2 'I don't know about that – even then. Obviously they can ask individually.'

SW 1 'I think there can be men who are equally sensitive in handling it.'

SW 2 'I'm not questioning the male's sensitivity.'

SW 3   'I think some of these things say more about the individual than they do about the male gender.'

Concluding Comments

The way in which child sexual abuse was responded to in the three authorities was similar in the following ways:

1. There were similar formal procedures in all areas.

2. There was commitment to joint interviewing and the development of closer liaison between social services departments and the police.

3. There was common agreement about the need for joint medicals where physical evidence of sexual abuse was *prima facie* likely to exist.

In short, the main lessons from Cleveland were being adopted.

In other ways, however, there were considerable differences in approach.

County's approach to child sexual abuse was most in line with Cleveland's recommendations and government guidance in all aspects apart from parental participation at conferences. Thus there was very close liaison with the police and a good deal of pre-investigative consultation before agreeing to follow up allegations and suspicions of child sexual abuse. Interviewing of children was kept to a minimum. The social services teams were actively involved in developing good inter-agency coordination between all agencies. The ethos of County's child sexual abuse work was very practical. Only those cases where there was a strong likelihood of affording the child better protection were vigorously pursued.

In Seacoast the quality of interprofessional relationships was more varied and there was generally greater divergence of views between professionals as to agreed courses of action. Some social services department social workers were still keen to conduct series of interviews with children whom they considered to be at risk in order to elicit some evidence. The continuation of this type of approach was very much against the trend supported by the Cleveland inquiry.

In City there was a much more varied approach, resulting to a large extent from a lack of clear policy development from the centre. Thus individual social workers tended to develop their own approaches, and it was not possible to characterize the approach of the child protection system as a whole.

These differences in approach will be considered throughout the chapters which examine in detail the progress of the 40 study cases.

CHAPTER 5

The Cases

In this chapter the 40 cases that form the main subject of the study will be considered, with emphasis on the range and types as far as they can be classified. As will be seen, there is considerable variety in the types of case that come under the heading of child sexual abuse, and indeed this is probably one of the reasons why it is so difficult to develop a systematic procedural response to this problem. That such variety is not just a feature of this study is borne out by the findings of Sharland *et al.* (1996), who found a similarly wide range of case types.

The intention of this chapter is to give an overview of the cases. In order to do this, they will first be considered in relation to a wider range of cases dealt with by the teams studied (i.e all those conferenced in one calendar year). This will provide evidence as to the 'typicality' of these cases for the areas studied. Second, some categorization of the 40 cases will be offered, along with case examples.

A Year's Sample

Child protection statistics for one year were analysed for each of the eight teams that were the subject of this study. For three teams the year selected for analysis was April 1988 to the end of March 1989, and for the remaining five it was April 1989 to March 1990.

Total Number of Child Sexual Abuse Conferences

Overall 98 child protection conferences were held about cases of child sexual abuse in the 8 teams studied in the years specified above. Forty-five (46%) of these resulted in registration and 53 (54%) were not registered.

Ages and Genders of Children

The ages of the children who were the focus of attention are set out in Table 5.1. As can be seen, there was an even spread across the age range. This overall pattern was reflected in the statistics for County and Seacoast. City had a much higher percentage of 12-year-olds and over than County and Seacoast among those who were the subject of its conferences. It should be noted that these are the ages of the children at the time of the case conferences, not their ages at the onset of abuse, which for some of the older children may have taken place at a much earlier age. Seventy-three per cent of the children about whom there were concerns were girls and 27 per cent were boys.

Table 5.1 Ages of children who were the subject of 98 child sexual abuse child protection conferences in one year in the three authorities

Age	No.
0–4	35 (28.4%)
5–11	52 (42.3%)
12–17	36 (29.3%)
Total	123

The Nature of the Alleged Abuses

The alleged abuses which were the subject of the 98 conferences are set out in Table 5.2. The terms used are taken from the criminal charges with which alleged abusers either were (or, more likely, could have been) charged by the police.

It will be noted that only 7 per cent of the cases involved incest, buggery and unlawful sexual intercourse. This could be interpreted as suggesting that the bulk of the work carried out by social workers and others is not at the serious end of abuse. However, such an interpretation would in all probability be fallacious. Indecent assaults include a wide continuum of activities ranging from a single attempt to touch a child sexually through to forced masturbation and oral sex. The records for the 98 cases reported here show that in some cases the concerns were about abuse that had been taking place for several years, while in others the concerns were about recent, more isolated events. Another point to note is the difficulty of assessing the nature of the sexual abuse in many

Table 5.2 Nature of the alleged abuse experienced by children who were
the subject of 98 child sexual abuse child protection conferences in one
year in the three authorities

Alleged abuse	No.
Indecent assault	51 (52%)
Schedule 1 offence	27 (28%)
Unlawful sexual intercourse/buggery/incest	7 (7%)
General concerns	13 (13%)
Total	98

cases. Some of the abused children were unable (or unwilling) to give detailed descriptions of what had happened – thus there was a general vagueness about the abuse incident or incidents. In other cases it was impossible to be sure that the children were giving complete details of what had happened to them. Clinicians suggest that in the initial stages of an investigation there is a likelihood that many abused children will play down the extent of their abuse.[1]

Despite these problems of clarification, however, the impression gained from reading the case records was that the bulk of the indecent assault cases involved abuse which was repeated and serious.

Just over a quarter of the cases which were conferenced involved the policing of Schedule 1 offenders who had either abused their own children on previous occasions or who had offended against children outside their own families, thereby raising concerns about the likelihood of harm to their own children. General concern cases largely involved younger children whose sexual behaviour allied to other indicators led to anxieties and suspicions about the standards of care being provided for them.

There was little difference between authorities in the pattern of abuses which were the subject of their conferences.

[1]   Furniss (1991) writes: 'We need to be aware that initial disclosures by children are very often only partial disclosures. Children come out with lesser abuse first before they trust to tell the full story, often much later. Some children initially say that they have only been abused once and they might implicate a stranger. Only later when they trust do they disclose long term abuse by friends, family members and fathers' (p.216).

The Families who were the Subject of Conferences

It was not possible to gain clear information about the socio-economic backgrounds of the families whose children were the subject of the 98 conferences. It was rare for any reference to be made to occupations in the case files. Using comments from records, it could be inferred that most of the families investigated were from poorer backgrounds.

Over half the families had been previously known to social services departments for child care concerns or needs. This finding is similar to that reached in Sharland *et al.*'s study (1996, p.35).

The family structure of the children who were the subject of the 98 conferences was available in the records. Table 5.3. gives the details.

Table 5.3 The family structure of the children who were the subject of 98 child sexual abuse child protection conferences in one year in the three authorities

Carer	No.
Mother/father	54 (55%)
Mother/step-father	12 (12%)
Mother/partner	16 (16.5%)
Mother only	11 (11.5%)
Father only	2 (2%)
Child in care	1 (1%)
No information	2 (2%)
Total	98 (98%)

National statistics (Central Statistics Office 1996) show that in 1991, 19 per cent of children were living in lone-parent families (in the North West the figure was much higher – around 30 %). The remaining 81 per cent were living in two-parent households, 9 per cent of which included step-parents. It is noticeable that there were proportionately fewer lone-parent families in the 98 cases about which information was gained than might be expected given the national figures. Children in these families were more likely to be living with adult males than was true of the general population.

There were no significant family structure differences between authorities.

Alleged Abusers

The alleged abusers in the 98 cases (or persons alleged to present risks to the children – as was seen in Table 5.2, 28 per cent of cases involved Schedule 1 offenders and 13 per cent involved general concerns about possible sexual abuse) are set out in Table 5.4.

Table 5.4 The alleged abusers of the children who were the subject of 98 child sexual abuse child protection conferences in one year in the three authorities

Abuser	No.
Father	46 (43%)
Step-father	9 (8%)
Mother's partner	15 (14%)
Uncles (including aunt's partner)	7 (7%)
Brother (including step- and -in-law)	10 (9%)
Grandfather	5 (5%)
Male cousin	2 (2%)
Mother	2 (2%)
Other female family members (aunt, sister)	2 (2%)
Neighbours	3 (3%)
Baby-sitter	1 (1%)
Not known	4 (4%)
Total	106

Note: There was more than one alleged abuser in some cases.

Sixty-five per cent of alleged abusers, including those presenting risks to children, were father figures living in the families. A further 22 per cent were other male members of the nuclear and extended families. Intrafamilial female abusers accounted for 4 per cent of the alleged abuse. Extrafamilial abuse accounted for only a small percentage of the whole.

The 40 Cases

Registration

Seventeen cases were selected from County, 13 from Seacoast and 10 from City. Exactly half were registered and half were not.

Gender and Age

The 40 cases involved 57 children who were either alleged to have been abused or were considered to be at risk of abuse. Twenty-three (40%) were male and 34 (60%) were female.

The ages of the children are set out in Table 5.5. Compared with the larger sample (Table 5.1), there are more older children in the study and a higher percentage of male children.

Table 5.5 The ages of the children in the 40 study cases

Age	No.
0–4	13 (23%)
5–11	20 (35%)
12–17	24 (42%)
Total	57

The Nature of the Alleged Abuses

Table 5.6 indicates the type of abuse included in the case study sample. This should be compared with Table 5.2.

Table 5.6 Nature of the alleged abuse of the children in the 40 study cases

Abuse	No.
Indecent assault	21 (52.5%)
Schedule 1 offence	6 (15%)
Unlawful sexual intercourse/buggery/incest	8 (20%)
General concern	5 (12.5%)
Total	40

The study sample differs from the larger sample by having fewer schedule 1 offender cases and more penetrative abuse cases.

Family Structure

The structure of the 40 families studied is set out in Table 5.7. This should be compared with Table 5.3.

Table 5.7 The family structure of the children in the 40 study cases

Carer	No.
Mother/father	15 (35%)
Mother/step-father	3 (7%)
Mother/partner	8 (18%)
Mother only	9 (21%)
Father/step-mother	3 (7%)
Father only	2 (5%)
Foster parents/care	3 (7%)
Total	43

Note. In 3 cases 2 families were involved.

More children were living in lone-parent families than in the wider sample. It was possible to gain more detailed information about the parents in the smaller sample, and it is notable that over half the children in this sample were living with only one of their biological parents. It should not be assumed from this that it is the non-biological parent within the family (if this is the family structure) who is necessarily the abuser of, or the danger to, the child. Rather, it seems as if children not living with both biological parents are more at risk of being sexually abused than those who do live with both.[2]

---

2   There is an extensive literature on 'step-father abuse', which tends to be used rather loosely as a term to describe all abuse of children by non-natal father figures in a household. Russell (1984) found from her sample of 930 women that 1 in 6 of those who had lived with a step-father at some time during their childhood had been abused, whereas the ratio of abuse for those who had lived with their natal fathers throughout childhood was 1 in 40. M. Gordon (1989), using reports from 17 American states, found that a third of all reported cases of sexual abuse were allegedly perpetrated by 'step-fathers'.

Data were collected about the overall number of children under 18 in the case study families. The average number was 2.5, which exceeds the national average size (1.8). However, only 7 families had more than 3 children (1 having 10).

Alleged Abusers

The alleged abusers (or adults seen as risks to children) are set out in Table 5.8, which should be compared with Table 5.4.

Table 5.8 The alleged abusers of the children in the 40 study cases

Abuser	No.
Father	17 (40%)
Step-father	4 (10%)
Mother's partner	4 (10%)
Uncle (incl. 1 step-uncle)	3 (7%)
Brother (incl. 1 step-brother and 1 brother-in-law)	3 (7%)
Grandfather/step-grandfather	2 (5%)
Friend/neighbour/lodger	5 (12%)
Foster-child/child in care	2 (5%)
Stranger	1 (2%)
Mother	1 (2%)
Total	42

The pattern is similar to that of the broader sample. One key difference is the fact that 4 of the abusers in the study sample were children under the age of 16.

Additional Information about the Study Sample

Some socio-economic information was available for the study sample which was not available for the wider sample. Information was gained on 32 of the 40 families about their extended families. Twenty-six of the 40 families had local extended families, whereas 6 described their sets of parents as living out of the region. Most of those with local families were in fairly close contact with them.

Just over half the parents were unemployed, a quarter were in paid jobs and there was no clear information about the remainder. Three of those who were employed had white-collar jobs. Generally, therefore, although most families in this study were from the lower social classes, not all were the kind of excluded poverty-stricken clients with whom children and family state social workers normally work. There were some very poor families of this kind and some whose living standards were of good quality. Seven of the families lived in owner-occupied accommodation.

Approximately three-quarters of the families had been in contact with social services departments previously. A third of these (10) had been involved as a result of more general children and family problems. Specific reasons for involvement included sorting out contact in divorce cases, children referred for running away, children with behavioural problems (usually referred by schools), children being bullied, children with disabilities, and families in need of general support and help. Twenty-two families had previously been in contact with social services departments because of child protection concerns (mainly child sexual abuse and general neglect).

General Comments about the Sample

The 40 cases which were selected at random – the main criterion being the availability of the researcher to attend child protection conferences at short notice – differed from the year sample in the following ways:

1. Slightly more registrations were recorded.
2. The children were on average slightly older.
3. There were more allegations of serious abuse.
4. Fewer children were living with both their biological parents.

Overall, however, the differences were not great. If anything, using the indicators above, the study sample seemed to be made up of more cases at the serious end of the spectrum found in the total sample for one year. It was argued in the previous chapter, using child protection return statistics, that the three local authorities in which the study took place represented a fair cross-section of authorities nationally. It is reasonable, therefore, to suggest that the cases on which this study is based are a fairly typical cross-section of the more problematic child sexual abuse cases that are dealt with by child protection systems across the country. It should be reiterated that these cases are those that the agencies chose to pursue more fully after initial investigation.

The Variety of Case Types

Having made the argument for the typicality of the sample *vis-à-vis* a year's work in the areas studied and (tentatively) nationally, it should be stressed again that the wide variation in case types was their most striking feature. I think this has been said

Category 1: Cases involving regular and continued abuse of one child (or two) in a family where the child seems to have been targeted to meet the sexual needs of the abuser

The criteria used for this category were repeated incidents of abuse over at least 6 months. Nine cases (11 children) fell into this category. Nine of the children were girls and two were boys. Their ages at the time of the allegations of abuse ranged from 7 to 16 (all but 3 were aged 12 and over). Alleged abusers included four fathers, two step-fathers, a step-grandfather, a brother and a brother-in-law. These cases included most of the serious offences in the sample – 3 cases of incest, 1 of buggery, 1 unlawful sexual intercourse and 4 indecent assaults. There were more convictions of offenders among this group than in any of the other categories. Registrations of children took place in five cases and in four cases children were placed in care. There was no obvious pattern in terms of the age of the abused child or of the relationship of the offender to the child (except that all cases were intrafamilial). As regards the age of the children, it should be noted that in some of these cases the abuse had been ongoing for several years. A 16-year-old girl said that she had been abused between the ages of 6 and 14 by her father. A 15-year-old girl said that she had been abused by her step-father since the age of 6. A 12-year-old boy said that he had been abused by his brother-in-law for 4 years.

CASE EXAMPLE: CHRISTINE[3]

Christine, aged 10, lived with her mother and two brothers, aged 17 and 18. Her mother told a neighbour that her older son had forced Christine to go into the toilet with him and had bruised her arms. The neighbour informed the school headteacher, who initially took no action. Two months later, following further concerns, she passed this information on to the social services department. A policewoman and a social worker interviewed Christine at a children's centre on two occasions. Christine alleged that her brother had had vaginal intercourse and oral sex with her over a long period of time. A medical examination was carried out after the second interview by a police surgeon and

---

3   All the names in the case examples are fictitious.

a paediatrician, but the findings were inconclusive. The brother was interviewed by the police and denied all the allegations. The police decided not to prosecute because of the lack of medical evidence, together with concern about the child's potential to act as a witness. All the professionals believed the girl had been sexually abused to some extent and they all believed that the brother had carried out the assaults. Christine's mother, who was partially sighted, was considered to be terrified of her older son, who was described at the conference as being 'large and aggressive'. Christine and her mother were placed in homeless accommodation after the second joint interview. The brother remained in the home. After three weeks he was barred from the house by an injunction taken out against him by his mother and placed in hostel accommodation. Christine and her mother returned home. Social work intervention followed for a period of six months with support given to the mother and therapeutic sessions provided for Christine. The brother had been imprisoned for theft offences during this time. Soon after the termination of social work involvement, he returned to the home. As a result, Christine was removed into foster-care on a place-of-safety order and remained there for five months. By this time the brother had left the home again and she was allowed to return. Care proceedings which had been initiated were dropped. After two years Christine was still at home with her mother and other brother.

Category 2: Cases involving regular and continued abuse of children in families where such abuse seems to be viewed as relatively normal

There are many similarities between the three cases in this and the previous category. The main difference is that more than one child was abused (or deemed to be at risk of abuse) in the families in this category. Indeed it seems that all female children in the households in this category were exposed to some form of actual or threatened sexual abuse. The other differentiating factor is that the mothers in these families seemed to be aware that abuse was happening and, for whatever reason, did not take obvious steps to protect their children. This is not to say that they necessarily condoned what was happening.[4] It is impossible without interviewing them directly to establish what

4 The issue of 'collusive' mothers remains a thorny one. There has been a tendency in the past to blame mothers for not adequately protecting their children. This derived to some extent from the contributions of family dysfunction theorists, as was seen in Chapter 2, and prompted strong reactions from feminist writers such as Macleod and Saraga (1988), who saw such mother-blaming as evidence of the extent to which male-dominated thinking dominated the problem of child sexual abuse. More recently there has been greater focus on trying to understand the reasons for mothers not intervening to protect their children.

their thought processes were. Reasons for non-protection could range from feeling powerless to intervene because of physical threat through to a sense of apathy and acceptance that what was happening to their children was the norm. There were three cases in this category involving four children in all. They were all female and their ages were 5, 7, 12 and 14. In one case, older female siblings had been abused and several years on had alerted the authorities about what had happened to them. They raised concerns about what they considered was happening to a younger sibling – the next in line. In the second case, a 14-year-old girl had been abused and reported that her 11-year-old sister (and, to a lesser extent, her 15-year-old sister) was at risk. In the third of these cases (involving the 5- and 7-year-old children) there were concerns about the potential abuse of all children in a large extended family, some of whose male members had been associated with a child sex abuse ring. The seven-year-old alleged that she had been raped by a family friend and the five-year-old alleged that she had been indecently assaulted by the same man. The three children in his family, aged five, three and one, were also thought to be at risk. In the other two cases the alleged abusers were the father and the mother's partner. The alleged abuses included unlawful sexual intercourse and indecent assaults. There was one successful prosecution in these three cases. None of the children in these cases came into care. All were registered.

CASE EXAMPLE: FRANCES

Frances, 14, who has a mild learning difficulty, alleged to a male lodger that she had 'had it' with her mother's boyfriend. The lodger informed the police who, either because it was at the weekend or because they were overriding the agreed procedures, or both, interviewed Frances at the police station and then arrested the boyfriend, who at this stage was no longer living with Frances'

sensitive to this self-blaming if they are to be helpful to mothers and children in these circumstances). On the other hand, not all mothers respond in this way to their children's allegations that they have been sexually abused. Bagley and Thurston (1996a) state that 'American studies indicate that up to a quarter of mothers do not accept their daughters as victims when [child sexual abuse] is revealed. This is especially likely when the victim is a young teenager when she reveals the incest, and when intercourse has taken place' (p.253). They are concerned about the impact that this has on the child or young person, based on the knowledge that the responses of non-abusing family members is of key importance to the long-term impact of child sexual abuse (see Beitchman 1992). Clearly, these are important issues and, as Waterhouse and Carnie (1992) point out, social workers and other professionals place considerable emphasis on the mother's ability to protect the child when making decisions about future risks. However, granted the problematic effect of such mothers' reactions, they are still understandable given the issues referred to above raised by Truesdell et al. (1986), and additionally because of the financial and other forms of dependency that marriage and partnerships can create.

CASE EXAMPLE: FRANCES

Frances, 14, who has a mild learning difficulty, alleged to a male lodger that she had 'had it' with her mother's boyfriend. The lodger informed the police who, either because it was at the weekend or because they were overriding the agreed procedures, or both, interviewed Frances at the police station and then arrested the boyfriend, who at this stage was no longer living with Frances' mother. Frances was the subject of a joint interview a few days after she had initially been questioned. She repeated her allegation at this interview, saying that she had had sexual intercourse with her mother's boyfriend on several occasions over the previous six months. She also made it clear that her mother knew what was happening. Frances had two sisters, aged 11 and 15. The mother's boyfriend had approached both of them for sex as well. It seems that the mother threw him out as a result of his making sexual advances to the 11-year-old. Following the interview, Frances was medically examined and the mother's boyfriend was charged with indecent assault, to which he was prepared to plead guilty. The standards of care in the home were very low, and it was felt as a result that the children should be registered and some support offered to the mother. Six months after the allegation was made, the mother's boyfriend was gaoled for 12 months and the mother received a formal caution. The mother by this time had another partner living in the home. The male worker attached to the case focused on monitoring the situation. No work was done specifically with Frances or other members of the family. The case was still open after two years and the children were still on the child protection register. The family had by this time moved to another local authority area.

Category 3: Cases where allegations of abuse were withdrawn after initial investigation

There were two cases in this category. The children could both have been placed in Category 1, but the fact that they withdrew their allegations during the investigation did have an impact on the way in which intervention was carried out, and separate categorization seems, therefore, to be useful. In one case it was strongly suspected that the child withdrew the allegations because she had been pressurized to do so by family members and in the other because she did not wish to cause further trouble. Both girls were aged 13. One initially made an allegation that she was currently being abused and the other initially made an allegation that she had been abused when she was five years old. The allegation in one case was of pressure to have sexual intercourse and in the other of oral sex with, and forced masturbation of, the adult. Although the withdrawal of the allegations meant that the criminal aspects of these cases were not followed up, social workers continued to work with the children and families concerned. Both children were registered, and in one case the child was made the subject of a place-of-safety order followed by care proceedings, resulting in a supervision order.

CASE EXAMPLE: CAROL

Carol, 13, told a teacher that her father had 'sex abused' her. The police and social services department were both notified. They contacted the mother and arranged a joint interview to be held at the school on the same day. The mother declined to be present at the interview, during the course of which Carol alleged that her father had forced her to have oral sex with him and to masturbate him when she was aged five or six. She said that there had been a recent incident (when her father made a sexual suggestion to her) which sparked off her memory of these events. The mother did not believe the allegation. The father was interviewed by the police and denied any abuse of his daughter. The police felt they had insufficient evidence with which to charge the father and so it was decided to take out a place-of-safety order on Carol. Carol was placed in a foster-home and went through a routine medical examination of the type carried out on all children coming into care. After four weeks, Carol withdrew her allegation. The professionals were of the view that she had done so because she realized that she was creating problems for her parents. Carol's name was placed on the child protection register (as was that of her 10-year-old brother). Despite the fact that she had withdrawn her allegation, and the fact that she returned home seven weeks after the initial investigation, the local authority decided to pursue care proceedings with a view to obtaining a supervision order. To some extent this decision was influenced by additional concerns about Carol's physical state (extreme thinness) and poor school behaviour. Also, she had expressed a view to the guardian ad litem that she wanted some formalized ongoing contact with the social services department. A one-year supervision order was made. Work was attempted with the family as a whole, but the father avoided contact. Focus gradually moved on to Carol's delinquent behaviour and her suspension from school. She and her brother were deregistered after a period of six months on the child protection register. At two years the case had been closed without any further contact following the expiry of the supervision order.

Category 4: Abuse of a child which was discovered at an early stage

This category includes four cases of alleged abuse where there does not appear to have been a long prior history, though it has to be stressed that this is not known for certain in any of the cases. In these cases the abuse is reported as being a one-off incident or, if more than that, of relatively recent occurrence, that is, within the previous three months. There were four cases in this category, involving four children (two boys and two girls). Two of the children were under 12. Alleged abusers included two fathers, an uncle and a step-brother. All alleged offences were ones of indecent assault, including touching over clothing, forced masturbation and oral sex. Two of the alleged offenders were successfully prosecuted. Two of the children spent periods in voluntary care as a result of the allegations.

CASE EXAMPLE: BERNICE

Bernice, aged four, told her childminder, who was a neighbour of the family, that her father played a game with her which involved her licking his willy. The story came not from a frightened child, but from one who was trying to gain attention in competition with other children who were in the house that day. The childminder informed Bernice's mother and then went to talk to her own mother. Following this discussion she contacted the NSPCC, who referred the allegation on to the social services department, who in turn involved the police. A joint interview was held in a suite specially equipped for video-recording. The child did not repeat her allegations. The father was away from home at the time of the allegation and was not due to return for a few days. This meant that no steps had to be taken to secure Bernice's immediate protection. Bernice was examined the next day by a police surgeon and a paediatrician. No evidence of abuse was found. The father was interviewed by the police on his return home. He denied the allegations, but was charged with indecent assault and bailed on condition that he have no contact with his children and that he live away from the family home.

A week after the first interview, Bernice was interviewed again by the police and social workers, and this time alleged that the abuse had taken place four times in the preceding six months. After about four weeks, however, the case against the father was dropped on the grounds that the child would not be a credible witness. Social workers remained involved in the case, supporting the mother in keeping the father away from the family home and offering some help to Bernice. The father returned to the family home on a permanent basis seven months after the initial allegation without the knowledge of the social services department workers, who had reduced their visiting by then. His return only came to light five months later. At this point it was felt that the father's re-establishment in the home was a *fait accompli*, and it was decided at a child protection conference to monitor the situation regularly. The family agreed to this. Two years after the initial allegation the children were still registered, social workers were visiting on a monthly basis and there were no further allegations of abuse.

Category 5: Families where sexual abuse of children is one of many care concerns

There were four cases in this category, which includes families where the initial allegation prompting a case conference was one of sexual abuse, but where general family problems relating to drug and alcohol abuse, mental illness and physical neglect were equally pressing problems. Five children in these four families were the main focus of concern (three boys and two girls). Their ages ranged from 1 to 13, with 5 of them being under the age of 12. Three of these children were placed in care as a result of the allegations. In two cases there were concerns that children were being inappropriately exposed to the sexual behaviour of adults. In one case a child was indecently assaulted by a non-family member in a local park. In another a father had allegedly indecently assaulted his daughter. No prosecutions resulted from these cases. There was some tension in the handling of these cases by professionals as to whether the sexual abuse should continue to be the main focus of attention or the wider problems of these four families.

CASE EXAMPLE: DARREN

Darren, aged nine, was allegedly sexually assaulted by a man in the local park. He told the police that he had spent the day with the man, who had given him money and alcohol and then had anally abused him. Darren told his grandmother what had happened. At that time he was living with her, because his mother was in a psychiatric hospital with drink and depression problems. The grandmother contacted the police, who in turn contacted the social services department. Darren was interviewed by police and social workers the next day at the social services department child protection suite. He changed his allegation, saying that he had not been anally abused but that the man had fondled his penis. The police suspected that the alleged abuser was a known paedophile, but were concerned about Darren as a credible witness, partly because he had changed his story and also because of his current behaviour. He had been excluded from school for eight months after making an arson attack on it. He had a reputation for being a wild child who roamed the streets a good deal and engaged in acts of vandalism. He was already known to the local social services department – his case was awaiting allocation at the time of the sexual abuse allegation. Darren was placed in care following the abuse allegation because his grandmother could not cope.

Over the next two years Darren initially went in and out of care and eventually, because of his behaviour in both residential care and at home, was made the subject of a care order. At one point he was placed in secure accommodation. Finally he returned home, and at the two-year point was still living there. Many efforts were made by social workers to provide Darren with some general therapeutic help, but with little success. There was no consideration of referring him for more specialized psychological/psychiatric help. Darren clearly had considerable problems that may or may not have been related to sexual abuse. It is most likely that there were a whole range of factors contributing to his behavioural problems, including his mother's psychiatric problems and reports of considerable conflict and violence within the home.

Category 6: Concerns about schedule 1 offenders living in the same households as children

This category is self-explanatory. However, it is worth pointing out that there were two main types of situation which concerned the child protection cases. The first was those cases where a Schedule 1 offender was known to be moving into a family where children were living. The second was those cases where a father living with his children was charged with offences against other children. There were 7 cases in this category, involving 15 children (7 girls and 8 boys), aged from 1 to 17. However, 10 of the children were aged 8 and under. In two cases father figures (one father, one mother's partner) were charged with sexual offences against individuals outside the family, and police referrals to social services departments led to an investigation of the home circumstances. In two cases males previously convicted of offences against children moved into families where there were children. In three cases fathers with sexual abuse offences either moved back to live with their children again (or in one case took sole care of his child).

CASE EXAMPLE: DAVID AND DESMOND

These two boys, one 7 and the other 12, lived with their mother and father. Both had learning difficulties. David (7) had a severe learning disability and was considered to be almost autistic. The children's parents were also considered to have mild learning difficulties. Concern was raised about the two boys following an allegation by the father's 35-year-old sister that he had been sexually abusing her since she was aged 18. The sister, who also had a learning disability, made the allegation to a worker at the day centre she was attending. The allegation was passed on to the social services department, which referred the matter to the police. The police interviewed the father, who admitted offences of incest and buggery. They decided, however, not to prosecute until the social services department had made an assessment of risk to the children.

Joint interviewing of the children was felt to be inappropriate, first because there had been no allegation of abuse of them, and second because of their learning disabilities.[5] An assessment of the parents was undertaken by a social worker who had some expertise in adult sex offender work. The main aim was to assess whether the father had paedophilic tendencies and whether the mother was deemed to be a protective parent. It was decided that the father was not a risk to the children, but that he needed work done with him on his sexual behaviour. He received a caution from the police and was referred to a social worker specializing in learning disability. It was also decided that the mother needed ongoing support and help with the care of her children.

Two years on, the social services department was still involved with the family. During this period, there had been concerns about the physical ill-treatment of the children, and the father had left home for a period, moving into another household where there were young children. This had prompted further concerns and a further assessment of him, this time by a forensic psychologist. By the end of the two-year period following the initial allegations the father had returned to the family home.

Category 7: Abuse of a child by another child or young person

There were five cases in this category. One of the cases could be seen as consenting sex between two young boys conducted inappropriately in public. However, this case raised a number of issues about sexual abuse and disability which will be considered in a later chapter. The 5 cases involved 5 male abusers, aged from 8 to 18, and 6 abused children (3 girls and 3 boys) aged between 2 and 15. In all but the case of the two boys mentioned above, the abuser was older than the abused. Three of the cases involved children in care as abusers and abused. The alleged abuses included oral sex, touching and exposure, attempted buggery and indecent assaults, one with violent threats. Only in one case was there a prosecution. These cases created a wide range of concerns, as the abusers were seen as being in need of some form of welfare intervention as well as those who were allegedly abused, which was clearly not the case with regard to adult abusers.[6] There were concerns about the backgrounds of the

5   Marchant and Page (1992) provide a very good account of how children with learning difficulties can be sensitively and effectively interviewed for child protection purposes. Key issues are the need for communication aids, skilled interviewers and for more time to be allowed for the completion of investigative interviews than would normally be required for children without disabilities.

6   Vizard et al. (1996) give an excellent review of the current issues surrounding child abusers. They point out that it is estimated that 20 per cent of all sexual abuse is perpetrated by adolescents (see Davis and Leitenberg 1987). However, they quote a study by Horne et al.

abusers and about whether they had been, or were being, abused themselves. Each of these cases in effect therefore became two cases.

CASE EXAMPLE: SEAN

Sean is 16. He had been in care for most of his life as a result of neglect and had spent the last nine years in the same foster-home. A two-year-old girl, the daughter of the foster-mother's neighbour, told her mother that Sean had involved her in oral sex. She informed the police and a joint interview was held with Sean at which he admitted the alleged offences. He was immediately removed from the foster-home and placed in a residential home. It was decided to interview all the children who had been in the foster-home while Sean had been living there. In the process, a six-year-old boy then living in the foster-home alleged that Sean had indecently assaulted him on several occasions. Sean was rearrested and admitted the offences. At the child protection conference it was agreed that prosecution of Sean should proceed and that he be referred to the regional forensic psychiatry service for treatment.

There was some suggestion that Sean had himself been abused several years ago by an older foster-child. Sean remained in residential care because his foster-mother no longer wished to care for him. In the three-month period following the conference there were further allegations against Sean – one of buggery made by a 3-year-old child living in the same foster-home and one of unlawful sexual intercourse with the 14-year-old daughter of the foster-parents. All these cases were dealt with through the courts, resulting in a supervision order being made on Sean. The contact with the forensic psychiatry service was not successful. Sean recommenced contact with his biological mother, but was still in care one year after the initial allegation was made.

Category 8: Abuse of children by separated parents while on access visits

There were three cases in this category. One was an allegation made by children to their mother; the second was an allegation made by children to their father about their mother's partner; and the third was an allegation made by a mother on the basis of concerns about her child's physical state on return from access visits to her father. Five children were involved in these three cases, aged three,

(1991) which found that, in Liverpool, 36 per cent of sexual abuse investigations involved alleged abusers aged under 18, including 2 per cent by children under the age of 7. The other key issues outlined by Vizard *et al.* are the lack of knowledge of normative pre-adolescent and adolescent sexual behaviour (see Chapter 1), which makes it difficult to assess what is and is not abusive; the links between being abused and being an abuser; the dangers of labelling young abusers versus the dangers associated with not responding seriously to their behaviour; and the lack of knowledge about the effectiveness of treatment.

four, six, seven and eight (three girls and two boys). The alleged abuse in one case was indecent assault involving masturbation and was unspecified in the other two. None of the children were registered. In none of the cases were the alleged abusers charged with offences. In one case the children were seen as too young to be credible witnesses and in another the mother was considered to be making a malicious allegation. In the third case there was considerable vagueness about whether abuse had taken place or not. In both cases where fathers were alleged to have abused their children, access was continued, but in one case it was required by the divorce court to take place under supervision.[7]

CASE EXAMPLE: AILSA

Ailsa, aged three, alleged to her mother that during an access visit to her father he had inserted his fingers into her vagina. The words she used were that he had 'pinched her halfpenny'. The parents were in the process of divorcing and therefore there was judicial involvement in the case already. Access to the father was suspended pending investigations into the alleged abuse. After an initial joint interview involving police and social services which yielded no evidence, a social services department worker carried out an assessment of the child which involved seeing her once, and occasionally twice, a week for two months. She repeated the allegations she had made to her mother to this social worker. Four months after the girl's allegation was first made, her four-year-old brother made a similar allegation. The same social worker again carried out a series of interviews (four in all). By this time, however, the court decided that it wanted a psychologist to conduct an assessment. However, the psychologist did not take up the case for over six months. Unlike the social worker, she video-taped the interviews she had with the children. She agreed with the social worker that Ailsa, though not necessarily her brother, had been abused.

The final hearing with regard to access was heard two years after the initial investigation. The judge was critical of the way in which the social worker had interviewed the children and of the fact that he had not used a video recording. He was also critical of the quality of the video recording carried out by the psychologist. He found that on the balance of probabilities the children had not been abused and decided on supervised access.

---

7   The term 'access' is used because intervention in this case preceded the implementation of the 1989 Children Act which introduced the term 'contact'.

Category 9: Concerns about an abused adult who has care of a child

There were two cases in this category. In the first there were concerns because of telephone calls made to a social worker by someone purporting to be a teenage girl who was being sexually abused by a family member. It turned out that the 'girl' was a woman who eventually disclosed that she had been raped by a stranger at the age of 12. This woman had a 3-year-old daughter. There were concerns about the mother's mental health and the care of her daughter.

The other case involved a 12-year-old boy whose biological parents were his mother and her father who had had a long incestuous relationship which had ultimately resulted in a prosecution. (This case was referred to in the Introduction.)

In neither case was there a concern that the child in the family was being sexually abused. Both were considered to be vulnerable because of the sexual abuse experiences of their mothers. In the 3-year-old's case there were some concerns about possible emotional neglect. In the case of the 12-year-old boy there were concerns about the impact on him of the knowledge of his parentage, and about how best to help individuals in the family manage the new situation. Both children were registered.

Category 10: Unlawful sexual intercourse between an adult and a consenting young person

There was one case of this type, involving a 15-year-old girl who was having a sexual relationship with her step-mother's brother, who was in his early 20s. The girl had been made a ward of court as a result of concerns about parental care several years before. There was some suggestion that the relationship with the step-uncle had started when the girl was aged 12, raising question marks as to the consensual–coercive dimensions of the relationship. There was no police investigation and the child was not registered.

Summary

These categorizations are problematic in some ways in that there is uncertainty in some cases about the veracity of the information. For instance, Category 4 (abuse of a child which is discovered at an early age) is based on the information given by the child to professionals which might understate the full seriousness and extent of the abuse that actually occurred (see Furniss 1991). In some cases the categorization is based on the interpretation and judgement of events by the researcher. For instance, Category 2 (cases involving regular and continued abuse of children in families where such abuse seems to be viewed as relatively normal) is based on accounts of family history given at conferences and on the reactions of parents to allegations as described by social workers. Similarly Category 5 (families where sexual abuse of children is one of many concerns) is based on the researcher's interpretation of cases. Category 10 (unlawful sexual intercourse between an adult and a consenting young person) is based on a judgement of a young person's view of a relationship which is derived not from the young person herself, but from the assessment of the professionals. The other categories are more factually based. Finally, as has already been noted, some cases could have been placed in more than one category.

Despite these difficulties, however, it is intended that this categorization will act as an aid to understanding the datnature/nurture

a presented in the following chapters. Brief details of all the categorized cases are presented in Appendix 1. These will be referred to in the following chapters where child protection work is analysed, according to their notation in Appendix 1; for example case (A5.2).

CHAPTER 6

Investigating Child Sexual Abuse

This chapter looks at how child sexual abuse referrals were made and responded to in the 40 cases which were the subject of the research. It has to be stressed again that these findings do not give a picture of how child sexual abuse referrals as a whole are responded to, as they were all cases that resulted in child protection conferences. Gibbons *et al.*'s study (1995) shows that 76 per cent of child sexual abuse referrals are likely to be filtered out prior to this stage. Cases that are filtered out in this way usually include a large number of children about whom suspicions of sexual abuse are aroused either because of sexually precocious behaviour or because of hearsay concerns (or both). Most of the cases in this sample commenced with allegations of abuse or with the presence of Schedule 1 offenders in the household.

In only three cases was neither of these criteria fulfilled. Nevertheless, they all seemed to justify concern and intervention. In the first of these there was a combination of factors leading to professionals being particularly concerned – vague allegations made by neighbours' children, sexualized behaviour of a child at school and generally deprived living conditions (Case A5.2). In the second, the father of two boys with disabilities was cautioned following his admission of a long-standing incestuous relationship with his disabled sister, and again there were concerns about general standards of care and material conditions in the family home (A6.6). The third case, which arguably need not have led to a full-blown investigation, involved a three-year-old child being cared for by her mother, who herself had been sexually abused and whose behaviour was giving professionals cause for concern that her child was also at risk of some form of sexual abuse (A9.1).

Initial Referrers

Table 6.1 identifies the initial referrers in the 40 cases. In just over half the cases the children themselves raised the first concerns about their abuse. In these cases they took the initiative to tell someone that they were being abused rather than it being detected by others (which is more characteristic of physical abuse and neglect referrals).

Table 6.1 The initial referrers in the 40 study cases

Referrers	No.
Children	22
Family members	6
Neighbours	3
Agency	7
Anonymous	1
No record	1
Total	40

Family members were rarely the first to raise concerns. In two of the six cases where they did, abuse was not proven and the referrers themselves (both mothers) and the standards of their emotional care of their children proved to be the real causes for concern (A8.3 and A9.1). In two of the remaining four cases, the family member referrers were women who had themselves been abused by the alleged abusers. In one of these cases, older sisters who had left the family home raised concerns about the risk to their younger sister who was still living with the parents (A2.3). In another the aunt of two young boys alleged that she had been abused by their father (her brother) and unwittingly raised concerns about their safety (A6.6). In the remaining two cases the referrer was, first, a mother alleging to a neighbour that her son was abusing her daughter (A1.2), and, second, a male lodger (not technically a family member in terms of kinship) alleging that the boyfriend of his landlady was abusing her daughter (A2.2).

Neighbours raised concerns in three cases (A1.4, A5.2 and A7.3). All alleged that their own children had been abused by the alleged abusers as well as the children in their households.

Referral of Schedule 1 offenders living in the same household came mainly through agencies (Category 6). The exceptions were in one case an anonymous call (A6.7) and in one case an employer to whom a customer had made a complaint following an assault on her child by one of the company's employees (A6.2).

Children 'Choosing' Whom to Refer to

Six of the 22 children who alleged that they were being abused told one or both of their parents. In two of these cases the alleged abusers were relatives not living in the same households as the children. In another the alleged abuser was a neighbour. In the three other cases, children made allegations to a non-abusing parent who was no longer living with the alleged abuser. All these referrals were, therefore, relatively safe ones because the parent referred to had no commitment to, or current involvement with, the alleged abuser.

Three children told relatives other than their parents. Three told non-related adults (a foster-parent, a neighbour and a friend of the parents). Two told friends of their own age.

Eight children told adults in positions of authority, including the police, schoolteachers (in two cases), a school caretaker, residential care workers (in two cases), a day centre worker and a childminder.

Four of the parents to whom the children made allegations immediately believed them. Two did not. The first of these two cases (A1.8) involved a 12-year-old boy who had been forced into an abusive relationship with his brother-in-law (aged 26) since he was aged 8. He was regularly anally abused during this period. He told his mother what had been happening to him after watching a television programme on male rape. She did not believe him at first and only went to the police two days later after talking to a friend about it. Two years before, the boy had made the same allegation to a friend of his mother who had passed the information on to her, but nothing further was done at that time.

The second case (A4.2) involved an 11-year-old boy whose adult step-brother had indecently assaulted him while staying at the family home. The boy told his step-mother what had happened, but she did not believe him. It was only after he had told another step-brother in the family (a month later) that the step-mother reluctantly decided to involve the authorities.

In all the other cases, those to whom the child made the allegations responded immediately. It was obvious in some cases that children had targeted persons whom they felt would do something, deliberately avoiding those whom they thought would not. A 12-year-old boy in a foster-home who had been sexually abused by the 14-year-old grandson of the foster-mother over a period of 15 months told the parents of a schoolfriend (A7.5). The foster-mother, when faced with the allegation, denied that there was any possibility that her grandson had done what was alleged.

For the children in these cases the allegations were successful in terms of alerting attention and getting someone to believe them. In two cases (A3.1 and A3.2) the allegations were later withdrawn, suggesting that the children who made them were uncertain about the consequences of bringing matters into the open, either for themselves or for their parents or both (for a fuller discussion of the issue of recantation, as it is termed in the USA, see Rieser 1991). However, as stressed above, all these cases were ones which resulted in conferences. Therefore, it is not surprising that the allegations were 'successful' as described.

Previous Referrals

It is interesting to note that in eight cases children had previously made allegations (or there had been strong suspicions that they were being sexually abused) without this prompting a response. Two cases have already been noted above (A1.8 and A4.2) – these two boys were unable to convince family members that they had been abused. In the remaining six cases the allegations had been made to professionals, including schoolteachers, the police, a residential social worker and a field social worker. In one case (A1.2) there had been three previous referrals that had not been responded to, two to social workers and one to a probation officer.

It is also notable that 12 of the cases had been worked with previously by child protection professionals as a result of child sexual abuse concerns. In other words they were at least 'second time round' cases, a fact which may have had an impact on the alacrity of the response this time. Another 18 cases had been previously known to social services departments for a variety of reasons – 7 for behavioural difficulties exhibited by children in school and at home; 3 for physical abuse; 3 were children who were already in care at the time of the abuse allegation; there was support for 2 families whose members had disabilities; and there was involvement with 3 families over divorce settlements involving children (including 2 matrimonial supervision orders).

Ten families had not been known to social services departments prior to the initial referral. However, at the time of the referral, four of these families seemed to have serious problems with child care over and above the concerns about sexual abuse and were known to other agencies. In one of these cases there was a serious drug problem; and in three there were concerns about poor standards of care and general deprivation, involving children with severe learning difficulties in two cases. It was hard to understand why social services departments had not been involved in these families earlier to help with these problems. In the remaining six cases it is unlikely that there would have been any need for state intervention or support, except for the allegation of sexual abuse.

Involving the Agencies

As demonstrated in Table 6.1, agencies raised their own concerns in seven cases. In three cases the originating agency was the police and they involved the social services departments. In two cases the originators were social services department social workers and they involved the police. In the remaining two, a health visitor and a school headmaster notified social services department workers of concerns that they had and these were in turn communicated to the police. Table 6.2 shows to which agencies/professionals the remaining 33 referrals were made.

Table 6.2 Agencies to which initial referrals were made by non-professionals in the 40 study cases

Agency	No.
Social services departments	13
Police	12
School	6
GP	1
Probation officer	1
Total	33

The referrals to social services departments had two characteristics. They were more likely to involve children at the younger end of the age range, and/or there was already some ongoing contact with social services departments (or contact in the recent past), which meant that there was some connection there already. These criteria accounted for all but one of the referrals to this agency. The fact that young children were more likely to be referred to social services departments possibly suggests that the main concern of those referring younger children was their welfare and protection.

Referrals to the police took place largely in respect of older children. In 9 of the 12 cases referred to them, the children were aged 12 or over. Referrals were made to the police in two ways: either as a result of a conscious decision on the part of a young person, relative or neighbour to take some action, or as a result of the police becoming involved with a family for some other reason, during the course of which allegations of sexual abuse were made. For instance, in one case (A1.3) a 16-year-old girl was seen fighting with her boyfriend in the street and the police picked them up and took them to the police station to sort matters out. The girl then alleged that she had been sexually abused by her father between the ages of 6 and 14 and stated that she was concerned that he was abusing her sister in the same way.

Referrals to schools involved children across the age ranges. The older children in this group clearly targeted a teacher as someone whom they could trust to handle what they had to tell them. In the case of all but one of the younger children, referrals were made to teachers by adults. The one exception was a girl, aged seven, who, during a conversation with the school caretaker, made a statement that her father was involved in sexual acts with her (it was not clear whether she was seeking help or imparting a fact of her life) (A1.7).

In two cases, other professionals were referred to, a GP and a probation officer. The former referred the case on to the police and the latter to the social services department.

Feelings about Involving Child Protection Professionals

The data for the referral processes were taken from files, from the information shared at child protection conferences and from interviews with social workers. Clearly these sources are second-hand and, therefore, the assessment of the motives and feelings of the actors involved is somewhat speculative. The impression gained was that in some cases the decision to involve professionals came about as a result of a good deal of thought and discussion on the part of friends, relatives and others. In other cases the referrals seemed to have been made more impulsively and there was little evidence of much preceding deliberation.

There seemed to be a good deal of ambivalence on the part of some of the older children about making a referral. Consider, for example, the following case involving a 14-year-old girl. Her father had already been convicted of gross indecency against her. She and her siblings had been placed on the child protection register and her father had been made the subject of a probation order. She told her friends at school that the abuse had started up again. They passed the information on to a teacher. The girl denied to the teacher that she was being abused, but nevertheless the social services department was contacted. Following interviews with the police and social workers, she disclosed that her father had abused her on several occasions and said that she had told her friends because she thought that he was going to force her to have sexual intercourse with him. At first, therefore, the disclosure seemed half-hearted and the girl was ready to retract it. Later on, however, it seems clear that she wanted something to be done to protect her (A1.5).

Indeed, apart from two young people who retracted their allegations soon after making them, most of the older children, including those who, like the 14-year-old girl just discussed, initially seemed reluctant to refer, eventually appeared relieved to have opened up about what was happening to them. It was not possible to evaluate the feelings of the younger children so clearly. For them, telling what had happened was not apparently accompanied by the feelings of ambivalence evident in the older children, probably because they were far less aware of the likely consequences of their allegations.

In the 18 cases where children were referred by others (without them first disclosing), such as family members or other agencies, it is difficult to know what they felt about the referrals. Nine of these children were aged ten and under. Two cases involved children who were over the age of ten but had severe learning disabilities. The seven remaining children, who were older, had no choice in the referral. They were not asked whether they wanted the investigation to proceed. To some degree they were treated as witnesses to a crime. In all these cases, however, these young people confirmed that they either were being, or had been, sexually abused.

The impression gained in most of these cases was that despite the pains and difficulties associated with the referral process, the children and young people in this study were not ultimately unhappy that matters had been brought to light. The following case (A1.9) provides an example of the type of response that these young people made in these circumstances. The subject of the investigation was a girl, aged 15. Her step-father had divorced her mother and left the family home four years previously. A neighbour of the family, who was being visited by a social worker, alleged to the social worker that her son had been sexually abused by this man just before he left. She also told the social worker that he was currently living with his second wife and two young children. As a result of this the social worker contacted the local police, who knew that this man had a history of sexual offending. Indeed, they suspected that he had sexually abused his step-daughter. It was decided to talk to her. It was put to her that there were concerns about her step-father's children's safety and that she could help by giving any information about his treatment of her. At first she was reluctant to help and denied that he had abused her. However, within three minutes of being interviewed she had burst into tears and begun to divulge to the policewoman who was leading the interview a long history of being abused between the ages of 6 and 12, starting with fondling and kissing and progressing to regular intercourse from the age of 9 or 10.[1]

Joint Interviews

Joint police and social work interviews were held in 25 of the 40 cases (62.5%). The main features of those cases which were the subject of joint interviews were (1) that there was a relatively clear allegation of abuse; and (2) that the alleged abuse was considered to be of a relatively serious nature. Thus all the cases in Category 1 (those involving regular and continued intrafamilial abuse of targeted children) were ones where joint interviewing took place. The majority of cases in Categories 2, 4, 5, 7 and 8 were also joint interviewed. Only one of the seven cases where there was concern about Schedule 1 offending resulted in a joint interview, and that was because in the course of a child protection conference a schoolteacher reported that a girl had previously made a rape allegation which had not been taken seriously.

Younger Children

Seven of the 25 children who were the subject of joint interviews were aged under 10. The age range of these children was between two and eight. Two of the children were interviewed twice by police and social workers. In the joint interviews, three of the children repeated the allegations that they had made earlier and four did not. Two of these, however, later repeated the allegations. One of these two was offered a series of sessions with a social worker during which she did indirectly repeat her allegation of abuse. The second, who had been made the subject of a protection order despite not making the allegation in a joint interview, made her allegation again at a later date and this time did repeat it in the subsequent joint interview.

1   The Cleveland Report (Butler-Sloss 1988) came to the conclusion that children's, and particularly young people's, wishes were being overridden by social workers and doctors carrying out child sexual abuse investigations there. The same criticism was made in the case of the Orkneys (Clyde 1992). However, as many of the cases in this study show, some very fine judgements have to be made about a child's wishes and feelings in deciding whether or not to proceed with investigations. While the assertion of children's rights following these two public inquiries has been an important reminder that children are not just 'objects of concern', nevertheless adopting a child's rights perspective does not in itself provide the answer. What it does is to ensure that these principles are not left out of the equation, but there is still a great deal of professional skill and judgement required in the decision-making process (see Smith 1997 for a discussion of these issues in relation to the broader child care field). This study does show that in the 40 cases examined, there were few incidents where children complained about the decisions to proceed. Roberts and Taylor's study (1993) would seem to confirm such a finding.

These interviews of younger children raised two main issues: first, in respect of their usefulness, and, second, in respect of their impact on the children. Only two of these seven cases resulted in prosecutions of the alleged abusers (both of whom admitted their offences), suggesting that the interviews had limited utility in this respect. From the social workers' point of view, most of these interviews were conducted reasonably sensitively. The police, who took the leading role in all the joint interviews (including those with older children), were perceived as being careful in their interviewing approach and non-threatening. One of these seven cases, however, did seem particularly insensitive to the needs of the child. This was a case of allegations made by a mother regarding the abuse of her eight-year-old daughter by her father (A8.3). The parents were divorced and the abuse was alleged to have been taking place on access visits. This was the ninth allegation that the mother had made over a four-year period. Despite the fact that most of the agencies were convinced that this child was not being abused (because she had never made an allegation and it was thought that the mother was imagining abuse or using these allegations to prevent her ex-husband having access to the child), nevertheless a joint interview was held and a medical examination carried out. Neither of these produced either an allegation or any evidence of abuse. Although the ensuing conference came to the conclusion that the mother was probably emotionally abusing her child by putting her through these ordeals (a form of Munchausen's syndrome by proxy – see Rand (1993) and Schreier (1996) for discussion of cases similar to this), there seemed to be a lack of understanding that the professionals had been to a fair degree colluding in this in the process of the investigation.

Older Children

Eighteen children who were joint interviewed were aged between 10 and 15. Full details were not available about all the interviews. However, one factor common to them all was that allegations of abuse were confirmed by the young people. Prosecutions of alleged abusers took place in ten of these cases, suggesting that in terms of utility, joint interviews of older children are more productive. Again using social work accounts of joint interviews, the pattern was the same as for the younger children, that is, the police took a lead role in the questioning. The social workers had relatively few complaints about the police in this respect. What criticisms there were centred on the way in which the police tried to substantiate evidence. For instance, in the case of one child who was recounting an abuse incident from several months previously, the police asked questions about what clothes she was wearing at the time, which was (1) difficult for her to remember, and (2) perceived by the social worker as a

Table 6.3 Venues for the joint interviews in the 25 study cases where interviews were held

Venue	No.
Social services department interviewing centre	5
Social services office	3
Police interviewing suite	2
Voluntary agency suite	3
Children's home	3
School	2
Police station	1
Hospital	1
Own home	2
Not known	3
Total	25

line of inquiry that the child experienced as questioning her veracity. Two children were said to have experienced embarrassment and difficulty in describing sexual parts of the body. This account by a social worker of an 11-year-old's experience provides a good example:

> M. actually balked at talking of the intimacies – not saying words like 'penis', but she did refer to private parts ... it was embarrassing for her, but her mother was quite helpful. She did refer to and clearly stated that her father had on many occasions stuck his finger and penis in her bottom and vagina ... as far as the police were concerned it was good evidence. (A1.3)[2]

2   There have been mixed findings in regard to police/social worker relations in child sexual abuse investigations. Both the Bexley Project (Metropolitan Police and London Borough of Bexley 1987), referred to in Chapter 2, and a study by Conroy, Fielding and Tunstill (1990) have commented on the development of good working relationships. Kelly and Regan (1990) take a more critical view, seeing this as an area that the police have taken over – their concern is that this could lead to less likelihood of the abuse (particularly of younger children) coming to light. Wattam (1992) sees developments such as the implementation of the guidelines in the Memorandum of Good Practice (Home Office 1992) as making

Venues for Interviews

The interviews were held in a variety of places, as Table 6.3 shows.

Less than half the interviews were held in specialized suites. The main reason for this was a shortage of such facilities in areas other than City, and there was a reluctance to make children and parents travel long distances in order to carry out interviews. The choice of venue was determined in some cases by what was seen as best for the child. Three children who were in care at the time of the allegation (or soon after) were interviewed in children's homes. Two were interviewed at schools. In one of these cases this was pre-planned because it was thought to be the best place for the child. In the other case, the joint interview took place on the same day that the allegation was made. The intention had been to interview a 13-year-old girl in a special suite. However, after the mother had been summoned to the school, it was decided that it would be best to deal with it there and then (A3.2). One 15-year-old girl was interviewed at the police station (A1.9). A joint interview had begun in the child's home, but during the course of the interview the child felt that she would rather talk to the investigating policewoman in a more confidential setting. She was eventually interviewed at the police station solely by the police officer. The social worker involved in this case did not feel that this was inappropriate in any way, because the girl had chosen both who should interview her and where it should take place.

In 15 of the 25 joint interviews, relatives were present as well as the children, police and social workers. In eight cases, the relatives were deliberately excluded, either because they were the alleged abusers or because the non-abusing parent did not believe the allegation that the child was making. In the case of the mother who was perceived as making wrongful allegations against the father (A8.3), she too was excluded. Apart from this case and one other where the sole parent was the alleged abuser, all the children who were joint interviewed without parents present were ten years old or more.

With regard to the 15 cases where children were not interviewed, there were a variety of reasons for not doing so. The main ones were that there were no direct allegations of abuse but rather general concerns, frequently because of the presence of a Schedule 1 offender in the household (nine cases). One

disclosures of abuse more artificial and less easy for children and young people, who have often carefully selected those to whom they wish to disclose information. The findings of the present study are, as has been pointed out, mixed: social workers were generally more supportive of the police than might be expected. Their key concerns were not that the police were less likely to discover abuse, but that they might be insensitive to the needs of the children and young people in the interviewing process, a fear that was borne out in only a small number of cases.

case was transferred from another district and so there was no need for additional interviewing of the child. In the remaining five cases there *were* allegations of abuse. However, in one case the child, who was aged six, had alleged that she had been assaulted by an eight-year-old child, and the police were not keen to pursue this matter further (A7.2). In another case (A3.1) an abuse allegation made by a 13-year-old girl was withdrawn very soon after it had been made. In a third case (A7.4) the abuse took place in residential care between two young people and the police were not informed until the conference was held, which was well after the allegation was first made. In the fourth case the young person making the allegation was the subject of wardship, and special permission was required to carry out a joint interview (A10.1). After consideration, this was not sought. In the fifth case (A8.2) the allegation made by a seven-year-old child was considered to be too vague. The main factors, therefore, in all the cases were either the age of the child, the lack of a clear allegation or both.

Medical Examinations

Medical examinations were held in 14 of the 40 cases (35%). Six of the children were examined by two doctors – police surgeons and paediatricians in Seacoast and City, and police surgeons and clinical medical officers in County. Eight children were examined by one doctor only (including three by their GP). Examinations were held in hospitals in Seacoast and City, and in police surgeon surgeries and health centres in County.

It is hard to detect any rationale for why some children were the subject of medical examinations and others were not. In the cases of all but two of the children who were given medical examinations there were clear allegations and joint interviews were also held. Nevertheless, this represents less than half of all such cases, and, therefore, does not point to a consistent connection with the seriousness of abuse. Similarly, there was no clear correlation between cases that were prosecuted and the use of medical examinations. Age did not seem to be a factor as the children who were examined were spread across the age range. One factor that might have influenced the use of medical examinations was the likelihood that they would produce evidence. This, however, did not seem to be the case either. For instance, two older girls who alleged that their fathers had abused them many months prior to the making of the allegations, and who were currently having sexual intercourse with boyfriends, were medically examined. Children who were not alleging anal or vaginal penetration were also examined. There are, of course, some valid reasons for wishing to give a sexually abused child or young person a medical in these circumstances: (1) to find out if there is evidence of abuse not alleged; (2) to check for sexually transmitted diseases; and (3) to provide reassurance to the child and non-abusing parent(s) that all is physically well. However, social workers felt that in some cases the police seemed automatically to require medical examinations. On the credit side, most also felt that things were beginning to change in this respect. This view was represented by one of the social workers as follows:

> That's been a recent change in our policy. I think in the past we've believed there's a tendency to have medicals just because an allegation has been made. There's been a few more recently where there's been an issue between us and the police. The issue for us is with girls. The police do want to have a medical to establish whether she's a virgin or not (for credibility) and we refuse on these grounds.

Children's Rights and Parents' Rights During Investigations

As has been stressed before, the views of the children and the parents in these 40 cases were not sought for this study (see, however, Appendix 2 for the views of a small number of parents from another study). This section draws mainly on the views of the practitioners carrying out the investigations and on observations gained from being present at the child protection conferences. The general feeling gained was that the investigation of child sexual abuse was reasonably conducted and welcomed by most of the children and non-abusing parents. Clearly some aspects of the process were upsetting for some children: the joint interviews, for instance, and the medical examinations. Nevertheless, there was little suggestion that the rights of children, in particular, were being disregarded (see footnote 1, p.94). Some younger children, particularly in Seacoast, were given a series of therapeutic/investigative interviews of the type that had been criticized in Cleveland. However, there was little suggestion of children being unduly pressurized. Indeed, the interviews may well have been seen as opportunities for play and special attention by some of the children. (It should be pointed out, however, that parents were not as happy with this type of intervention, an issue which will be expanded upon in the next chapter.) The overall impression gained about the older children in this study was that for the most part they clearly wanted to get something done about their situation.

With regard to joint interviewing, the vast majority of the interviews in this study took place prior to the implementation of the guidance provided by the Memorandum of Good Practice. The joint interviewing in much of this study would not have met the new criteria in terms of consistency and standard of evidence. However, one of the positives of this approach was that it allowed for a good deal of flexibility on the part of the professionals as to how and where the interviews took place. Only four of the interviews were video-recorded and in only two of the cases were children ultimately required to give evidence in a criminal prosecution (both of which resulted in not guilty outcomes). It could, of course, be argued that improved interviewing at this stage in terms of gathering evidence might have improved the successful prosecution rates. However, the findings of Social Services Inspectorate research (SSI 1994) are not encouraging in this respect. The overall impression gained was that social workers were being very careful to respect children's wishes as far as possible and were sensitive to their needs in most of the cases observed. Similarly, there seemed to be few complaints about police involvement at this stage.

Paying due attention to the rights of parents to be fully informed of the process of investigation was considered to be virtually absent in Cleveland. The practice observed in the authorities in this study provides a more mixed picture. Most non-abusing parents, particularly those who believed and supported their children, were normally fully involved in the process of investigation, despite the fact that most did not attend child protection conferences (see next chapter). This was true in 28 of the 40 cases.

However, in the remaining 12 cases, parents were not immediately informed of concerns for a variety of reasons. In one case (A1.7) the lone parent (male) of a child was the alleged abuser. It was decided to protect the child first by use of an emergency order and then to inform him of the concerns. The child in this case was seven years old and hinting that she was being subjected to sexual intercourse. In another case the mother was considered to be complicit in the alleged abuse, and in two others it was the behaviour of the mothers that was giving most cause for concern. In two other cases, the mothers were seen as unprotective. In three cases, the young people making the allegations were in care at the time – in one of these cases the parents could not be contacted. In the other two the parents were simply not informed until after the joint interview, because there was some reason for believing (based on their reaction to previous crises) that their responses would not be supportive. There were three other cases where conscious decisions were taken not to inform parents immediately of concerns.

In the first of these cases (A8.2), a boy (seven) and his sister (six), had alleged to their father, who was divorced from their mother, that her boyfriend had come into their bedroom and pressed himself against them. In the boy's case this was reported as if it had happened in a nightmare. The father referred the matter on to the social services department, which had just been contacted by a headteacher who had serious concerns about the boy's difficult behaviour in the classroom. The social services department social worker tried to contact the mother, but she was not available. So, in the social worker's words, 'I sent her a letter that day when I got back to the office, saying that the school had been in touch and that there was a case conference being arranged, and that I'd quite like to meet her to discuss any concerns that she might have and any concerns that the school has expressed.' The social worker thus led the mother to believe that the concern was in respect of the boy's school behaviour. The social worker was not happy with the deception:

> Mark [the team leader] and David [the child protection consultant] had discussed it. I've asked to do play sessions with the kids, but we weren't sure about being heavy-handed with a sexual abuse investigation at that stage. I don't know if I'm happy about it at all, because again you're not up front, but what was felt from school and everyone was that Jane [the mother] wouldn't cooperate if we came in heavy-handed ... What we hoped was that it would come out in the play sessions and then we could pick it up with mum and Patrick.

In fact the mother was only informed about the professionals' concerns at the end of the case conference, which was held soon after the initial allegation was made. The deception worked against progress. In the aftermath of the conference, the mother was said to be initially shocked and then very angry about the way in which the social services department had handled the matter.

In the second case, involving a 15-year-old girl who was received into care because she was refusing to go home, the police wanted time to prepare an interview with the father, who she had alleged had sexually assaulted her. The social workers informed the parents that she had alleged that the mother had physically ill-treated her. Conflict with the parents persisted throughout the duration of this case (A4.3).

In the third case, involving a 12-year-old boy with a learning difficulty who was considered to be the initiator of an indecent act with an older boy, the parents were informed that there was going to be a case conference and asked to attend at the end. However, they were not told of the reasons for the conference being held until they finally went into the conference. There was some concern that the boy may have been exposed to pornographic videos which his father possessed and possibly that the father might be abusing him in some way. These suspicions proved to have some justification, as six months later the adult daughter of this man alleged that he had sexually abused her throughout much of her childhood (A7.1).

On the whole, setting aside the question of ethics, the deceptions did not prove to be useful. In addition, the social workers were not happy operating in this way unless there was a clear reason to believe that being open about the alleged abuse would place the child at further risk. Social workers seemed to be happier using more straightforward approaches. As one social worker put it: 'My policy with this family, although I get flak, and I think the reason that I still get in there is that despite how they blow up and all the names they call me, I persist in telling them everything that I am doing, why I'm doing it, even if they don't like it' (A4.2).

Concluding Comments

In this chapter the focus has been on the referral process and the initial investigation of allegations. The general picture that emerges is that older children tend to select someone who they feel will take the right action on their behalf. Younger children are more likely initially to raise concerns by their behaviour or demeanour. It was pointed out that all the study cases were 'successful' referrals in that they aroused sufficient concern among professionals to result in child protection conferences. There are likely to be many cases referred which do not get taken up properly for a variety of reasons. It is worth noting that these successful referrals include a high number of cases where abuse had allegedly been ongoing for some considerable period of time. There was also evidence in some cases of previous unsuccessful attempts to refer. Many of the families from whom the referred children came were already known to social services departments for child protection or other reasons.

The majority of the investigations seemed to be reasonably well conducted and sensitive to the needs and wishes of children in particular and, to a lesser extent, to those of the parents. With regard to the latter, much depended on whether they were implicated in the abuse or did not believe or support the child. The demands of the system in respect of the requirements of joint interviews were less rigid than is true of the current situation, and in the majority of cases, particularly those involving younger children, parents were allowed to be present at them. Medical examinations were held in a minority of cases and the pressure to have them (usually from the police) was diminishing.

On the negative side, parents were not properly informed of the true concerns of the professionals in a small number of the cases. There was also evidence of unnecessary interviewing and medical inspection in one or two cases.

CHAPTER 7

Protecting Children and Helping Families
The Child Protection Conference

This chapter considers the way in which decisions were reached at child protection conferences about how best to protect children in the 40 families which were the subject of this study. As has been pointed out before, it should be noted that these 40 cases were among those considered the most serious of all referrals and that decisions are reached on what are seen to be less serious cases in a much more informal way, usually by either the police or social services alone or after brief consultation with each other.

As will be seen, the reality of intervention and decision-making was far more complex than suggested in formal guidelines. The main model of intervention to be found in the procedure manuals of all three areas was discussed in Chapter 3. In summary, the expectation was that all allegations of child sexual abuse should be jointly discussed by police and social services department personnel and that in those cases which they considered sufficiently serious, joint interviews should be conducted, along with joint medical examinations where appropriate. Interdisciplinary child protection conferences should follow these investigative activities to determine future courses of action.

The practice was in fact far different from the theory. This is particularly emphasized by data on the timing of the conferences in relation to the making of the referrals. According to the 1988 Working Together guidelines (DHSS 1988), which were largely endorsed by the recommended procedures in the three study areas, the maximum time-gap between initial referral and the child protection conference should have been eight days. This was extended to 15 days by the 1991 guidelines (DoH 1991a) under which some of the later cases were conducted. Table 7.1 shows that there was very little adherence to these time limits in the 40 cases studied.

Table 7.1 Time-gap between investigation and conference in the 40 study cases

Time-gap	No. of cases
Up to 15 days	11 (27.5%)
16–28 days	11 (27.5%)
29–56 days	9 (22.5%)
57–84 days	3 (7.5%)
85–112 days	3 (7.5%)
Data unavailable	3 (7.5%)
Total	40

Thus in only about a quarter of the cases were the recommended timings achieved. In fact, the average time-gap between initial allegation and conference was 39 days, and the range was from 2 to 112 days.[1] There were some differences between authorities in this respect. Seacoast was most likely to hold conferences within 15 days of the allegation being made. On the other hand, none of City's conferences were held during this period, and on average City took much longer to hold conferences than Seacoast and County.

As will be seen, this wide variation in the timing of the conferences resulted in their having very different functions – some of those that were held soon after allegations were made acted as pre-intervention strategy meetings, and some of those held several weeks after the initial referrals acted as after-the-event formalizing of decisions taken on the ground by child protection professionals some time in the past. The focus in these cases was on accountability as much as it was on those functions which are normally associated with child protection conferences, that is, decision-making and

---

[1]   Thoburn *et al.* (1995) found a good deal of variation in times between allegations and initial conferences in their study of all forms of child protection cases. The variations were not, however, as wide as in this study. Thirty-seven per cent of conferences took place within 14 days of the allegations being made and 36 per cent took place over 21 days after the allegations were made (see pp.34–35).

planning.[2] It was notable, however, that there was a close correlation between holding conferences relatively early and decisions to place children's names on child protection registers. Fifteen of the 20 registered cases were subject to conferences held within 28 days of the referral. This suggests that, by and large, the more pressing cases were dealt with with greater urgency.

Where the Conferences were Held

Twenty-eight of the 40 conferences were held in social services department offices and six in other social services department settings (four in an old people's home and two in a children's home). Two conferences were held in a hospital and one in a city solicitor's office. Had the focus been on physical abuse it is likely that more conferences would have been held in hospitals. However, even allowing for this, the predominant siting of conferences in social services settings reflects the extent to which social workers are now responsible for child protection work in general, and for child sexual abuse cases in particular. It similarly reflects the diminishing responsibility of hospital-based medical personnel in this area of work.

Who Attended

On average there were 10.2 people (predominantly professionals) at each of the 40 conferences. The smallest conference had 6 attenders and the largest 21. Table 7.2 gives the details of those who attended all the conferences.

Professionals

As has been commented on in previous research on child protection conferences (Corby 1987; Farmer and Owen 1995), there are regular and occasional participants at these meetings. The regulars include the chairs and secretaries, the police, and health visitor and social work managers. The situation varied with regard to the police: in County the police were organized in specialist teams, whereas in Seacoast and City what specialization there was was largely informal. Therefore, the police were more likely to be regular attenders at County's conferences than was the case in Seacoast and City. In one of the Seacoast areas, a borough solicitor was present at all conferences, and, therefore, was part of the regular group in that area.

---

2   Farmer and Owen (1995) found similarly, and argued that the child protection system in general, and child protection conferences in particular, were geared to the needs of the professionals as much as to those of the children.

Table 7.2 Attenders at the 40 child protection conferences

	Total No.
Professionals	
Chairperson	40
Secretary	40
Social work managers	47
Social workers	54
Police officers	52
Health visitors/managers	39
Schoolteachers	48
Education welfare officers	18
School nurses	16
Local authority solicitor	11
Clinical medical officers	10
Probation officers	9
GPs	8
Residential social workers	6
Housing officers	5
Foster parents	2
Play group workers	2
Nursery nurses	2
Paediatricians	1
Police surgeons	1
Total	411
Family Members	
Mothers	6
Fathers	2
Grandmother	1
Total	9

For regulars, the conferences were more routine matters than for the occasionals. They were like court officials in court settings – *au fait* with the
procedures, familiar with other key actors and generally more comfortable
with the conference process.

The occasionals were more closely linked to the events that had happened
and to the characters that were involved in the abuse situations. Social workers,
though key participants, could still be considered to be occasionals because
most attended only a few child protection conferences in any one year. Judging
from the responses of some of the social workers who were interviewed in
groups, the likelihood was that in the case of child sexual abuse conferences
they would be even less involved than that. Non-social work occasional
professionals were probably even less likely to be involved in cases of child
sexual abuse.

The preponderance of schoolteachers attending child sexual abuse conferences reflects the age range of the children who were sexually abused. While
some of these teachers were directly involved in the child abuse allegation
process, most had no prior connection with the sexual abuse aspect and were
present because they were required to give general information about children.
The number of education welfare officers involved reflects the more general
problems that many of the families which came into the system were experiencing. The same could be said of the involvement of probation officers,
whose presence in most cases was not specifically as a result of the alleged
sexual abuse, but because family members were involved in criminal activity.

Very few medical personnel who had been involved in the initial investigations attended the conferences. The main exceptions were community
medical officers, who were particularly involved in child protection work in
County, where hospital services were less immediately available. GPs attended
about 20 per cent of conferences.[3]

Relatives

Relatives attended only 7 of the 40 conferences, and only 3 of these right
through to the end. Seacoast and City had a policy of inviting parents to attend
at the end of conferences which by late 1991 they had extended to attendance
throughout. County did not invite parents to attend conferences at all. In

---

[3]   GP attendance at child protection conferences was for many years reported as being much
       lower than this. However, Farmer and Owen (1995) report attendance at 25 per cent in their
       study of all child protection conferences. By and large, GPs would be expected to have a
       more direct role in physical abuse and neglect cases than in cases of child sexual abuse.

Seacoast and City, parents were invited to attend all review conferences throughout.

For the most part, these practices reflected what was happening throughout the country at this time (see Chapter 2, footnote 6). After a long period where non-attendance of parents at child protection conferences was considered to be the norm, the 1988 Working Together guidelines (DHSS 1988) (following on from the recommendations of the Cleveland Report) advised that parents should attend conferences, provided such attendance was seen not to act against the best interests of the child. The 1991 Working Together guidelines (DoH 1991a) placed more onus on conference personnel to justify the need for exclusion of parents and children who were of sufficient age and understanding. Nevertheless, in many areas it took time for authorities to adjust to central government guidance.

The involvement of parents (and, to a lesser extent, children) is now the norm (see Lewis 1992), and there are differing accounts about the benefits of this new development in terms of parental participation and empowerment.[4]

It must be stressed that the parents who were observed at the initial conferences in Seacoast and City were not required to participate to any great extent. Most were informed of decisions reached and were asked to give their responses. There was more involvement of parents at review conferences – usually these were non-abusing parents who were working cooperatively with professionals. It should also be borne in mind that the fact that the bulk of conferences were not attended by parents meant that their form and content may well have been to some degree different from that of those taking place at the present time.

---

4   Studies carried out into parental participation at conferences since 1992 (see Thoburn *et al.* 1995) have largely seen the development as a worthwhile one which has been welcomed by professionals and parents alike. Separate research carried out by myself and colleagues has cast some doubt on what this type of participation is achieving (Corby *et al.* 1996). Certainly many parents interviewed in the aforementioned study were unhappy about their experiences of being involved (see Appendix 2 of this book). Some effects of parental participation at child protection conferences, however, are less disputed. Conferences have probably become more formalized in their presentation as a result of parents being present. It is less likely now that professionals will dispute courses of action and decisions made by other professionals during initial investigations in front of parents at conferences. It is also more likely that professionals will be more careful about how they comment about families (in their presence) during conferences. Conferences are more likely to take place in situations where relatively clear decisions can be reached, and are now less likely to have the function of strategy meetings. Such communications and negotiations between professionals are likely to take place elsewhere. These factors need to be taken into account when considering the form and process of the conferences reported on in this study.

Chairing of Conferences

Seven chairpersons presided over the 40 conferences attended, all of whom were experienced in chairing such conferences on a regular basis. Seacoast, at the time of the research, had retained a system of line managers chairing conferences, whereas City and County used non-line manager child protection specialists. Assessing the quality of chairing is a very difficult task and it is even more difficult to determine what sort of influence it has on outcomes (see Lewis 1994). Being a line manager in itself did not seem to have a negative effect in this study. The Jasmine Beckford inquiry (London Borough of Brent 1985) recommended that chairpersons should not be line managers because of the potential dangers of being too closely involved with front-line workers which could affect objectivity. However, much seems to depend on the professionalism of the individuals involved. One of the line manager chairpersons seemed to have kept his child protection knowledge well up to date and to have retained a sense of objectivity. He was well respected by social workers in his area for his rational approach to the work. The lack of clarity of planning referred to above was not confined to conferences chaired by line managers.

Chairing styles varied from being authoritative to more democratic. Some chairpersons saw themselves as having expertise in the field and considered that their role was to use this expertise to influence conference decisions. Others were less likely to lead in this sense and tended to concentrate on seeking out a consensus from the conference participants. However, the style adopted by the chairperson did not seem to be a key factor in the effectiveness of the conferences. The most important factor seemed to be the degree of security that a chairperson provided to conference members. This element was checked out with social workers only. They seemed to put great weight on the chairperson's impact and on whether they felt them to have a 'safe pair of hands' and an objective approach. In their view, chairing child protection conferences required a range of skills, of which the most important were: (1) the ability to manage inter-agency conflicts and disagreements, and to encourage people to work together; and (2) the ability to summarize a complex set of facts and opinions and draw out from them a coherent and practical plan of ongoing intervention.

The Length of the Conferences

Conferences in this study lasted on average 57 minutes, the range being from 20 to 105 minutes. There were no obvious differences between the three authorities in this respect. The wide variation in time may reflect the range of functions that the conferences were encompassing.

The Functions of the Conferences

As stressed earlier, child protection conferences can, particularly depending on their timing, serve a variety of functions. In the 40 initial conferences which were the focus of this study, the following functions were observed:

- discussing information and concerns about a child

- deciding whether further investigation was needed and, if so, how it should be carried out

- reviewing the events of an investigation and tying up loose ends

- sorting out disagreements between agencies about the way in which child protection investigations were carried out

- deciding on future plans – including further assessment, strategies of intervention, agency responsibilities, and so on.

These functions will now be used as a framework for analysing the decision-making process at the conferences.

Sharing Information about Children and Families

Sharing information between professionals has traditionally been seen as a key function of child protection conferences and was one of the main activities in all the conferences observed.

In some of the conferences, the information shared by social workers about the nature of the alleged abuse made professionals such as GPs and school-teachers see families' (and particularly children's) behaviours in a different light than before. Children who were previously seen by teachers as devious, difficult and challenging were now seen as vulnerable and abused. Such revelatory insights did not always result, however. Some of the information given by teachers seemed ridiculously out of place in the context. In the case of a 14-year-old boy whose father had persistently buggered him, the school-teacher reported that he was an able child, but that he tended to be careless, chatty and to put little effort into school work – a clear case of wearing occupational blinkers!

What was very apparent from the information shared at conferences was the high degree of general deprivation experienced by a sizeable minority of the families who were under scrutiny (13 out of 40). Their general problems and difficulties were already known to various professionals before the concern about sexual abuse triggered off the need for coordinated intervention. With hindsight it was surprising that these families were not receiving more intensive help, support and monitoring from health and welfare professionals prior to the sexual abuse allegations.

Another striking factor was the number of references made at conferences to behavioural/emotional problems demonstrated by children before the allegations of abuse were made (14 in addition to the deprived families referred to above, some of whose children were also demonstrating behavioural difficulties). These behavioural problems, usually observed in school, may of course have been symptoms of being sexually abused. Nevertheless, the lack of a more concerted response from professionals at an earlier stage was again surprising. In seven families (including six of the above) children had learning difficulties (five moderate and two severe). It is notable that in only 11 of the 40 families was sexual abuse the sole known problem, judging from the accounts given by professionals at the conferences.

There were many negative comments about family members (including children) at the conferences attended. Some alleged abusers were described as 'perverts' and seemed to arouse general disgust. Some mothers were described as 'ineffectual'. As pointed out above, some children were negatively portrayed by schoolteachers, despite the knowledge of what had happened to them. Such negative framing was largely dysfunctional. Although it allowed professionals to let off steam, in terms of deciding future courses of action it had a very limited effect. The presence of parents clearly inhibited this negative framing. It was evident even from the small number of occasions that the parents attended conferences in this study that professionals were more likely to focus on facts and less likely to put forward their opinions because of this. Now that parental attendance is much more the norm there is likely to be further improvement in this respect.

Deciding Whether Further Investigation was Needed and How it Should be Carried Out

This was the main function in ten conferences, most of which were held very soon after the initial referral. As pointed out previously, conferences in these cases took the form more of strategy meetings. Parents were not directly involved in the main body of these conferences. They came in at the end of two of them, simply to be informed of outcomes. Social workers said that all the parents in these cases knew that conferences were taking place. However, they were not always told what the particular concerns of the child protection professionals were. This was true in 2 of these 10 cases, both of which were discussed in some detail in Chapter 6 (A7.5 and A8.2). The degree of secrecy used in both these cases was questionable.

Five of these conferences were concerned with cases where Schedule 1 offenders were living in the same household as children. Their main function was to decide whether there was sufficient concern about these offenders' behaviour to warrant investigating the safety of children living with them. It was agreed to follow up two of these cases. In the first of these it was revealed at the conference that a 15-year-old girl in the family had alleged that she had been raped in the past by someone outside the family who was now dead (A6.2). As a consequence it was decided to conduct a joint interview with her. In the second case (A6.5), it was decided to seek a supervision order without jointly interviewing the children concerned. Several factors contributed to this decision: the children were all very young, the person giving cause for concern had been convicted of offences fairly recently, and neither he nor the mother cooperated with the social workers in any way. In two of these schedule 1 cases it was decided not to take further action – in one of these the offence which was discovered had taken place many years previously (A6.1), and in the other it was felt that the father was not a risk to his child (A6.4). In the last of these five cases it was decided that social workers should remain involved with the family without carrying out a formal investigation (A6.7). It was questionable whether in fact full child protection conferences were really necessary in these last three cases. Decisions could have been reached at a more informal level.

There was clearly a need to involve all relevant professionals in the planning of intervention in two cases in this category. In the first of these, the alleged abuser was suspected of being involved in an organized abuse ring (A2.1). In the second, the issue was one of a case of long-standing incest requiring a particularly careful and thought-through approach (A9.2). It was understandable that professionals needed to share concerns and views before taking matters further in these cases, and in these circumstances the holding of a child protection conference before taking action seemed appropriate.

On the whole, however, greater use could have been made of strategy meetings involving key agencies rather than full conferences in most of the cases referred to above. Holding pre-conference strategy meetings had been part of County's formal procedures for some time and was being implemented in City towards the end of the study period. In Seacoast such preliminary planning was not placed on a formal footing throughout the period of the research.[5]

---

5   The Cleveland Report recommended the setting up of interdisciplinary Strategic Assessment Teams for dealing with problematic cases of suspected child sexual abuse (Butler-Sloss 1988, pp.249–51). I am not aware of any Area Child Protection Committee that has formally established such teams. Many authorities, like County, have a procedure for

Reviewing the Events of an Investigation and Tying up Loose Ends

Some conferences, as pointed out in an earlier section of this chapter, took place a long time after the initial investigation. Often key decisions had been made by the time of these conferences and their main function was to rubber-stamp those decisions to the satisfaction of all agencies.[6] This was the main function of five of the observed conferences. By the time they were held, the main investigative work had been completed and children were no longer seen to be at risk. In most of these cases, there seemed to be very little justification for the length of delay. The following case is a good example of this. There was concern about a seven-year-old boy whose step-father was accused of sexually abusing a young girl who was the daughter of family friends (A5.2). There were also concerns about the boy's sexual behaviour at school. The case had been investigated following two strategy meetings and then nothing further had happened. The mother had been concerned because she thought that her son was going to be removed from her care. She had leaned heavily on her health visitor, who had a lot of concerns about the family. It was only as a result of pressure from the health service that a conference was finally held. The investigation had in fact been closed by the social services department workers because of lack of clear evidence and a firm allegation. However, other professionals and the parents had not been informed.

In four cases, it was not very clear why the conference needed to be held at all. The fact that sexual abuse had been confirmed in all of these cases (and in

pre-conference consultation – however, most of the interprofessional consultation in the 40 cases considered here (including that in County) took place in a relatively informal way and mainly consisted of discussions between the police and social services department personnel. Ironically, the Orkney Report (Clyde 1992) was critical of the fact that a child protection conference was not held prior to taking action in that case – decisions were reached at strategy meetings between police and social workers. In the current climate, where there is greater emphasis on openness and working in partnership with parents, the issue of pre-conference liaison has become even more problematic. The Working Together guidelines do not offer any clarity on this score.

6   There were good reasons for delaying initial conferences in a small number of cases, as the following examples show. In one, a strategy meeting held on a man whose sister had alleged he had abused her had agreed for the need for an assessment of him in order to be sure that he was not a risk to his own children (A6.6). The assessment carried out took three months to complete and involved weekly visiting of the parents (including joint and separate inter-views). The aim of the assessment was to explore the man's sexual views, to examine his sense of responsibility for the abuse of his sister, and to extrapolate from the findings as to the degree of risk he presented to his children. In another case, involving abuse by a 16-year-old foster-child, it was thought necessary to interview all the foster-children he had been in contact with before taking decisions about future action (A7.3). A third case involved the mother of a three-year-old child (A9.1). This woman was thought to be pretending, via anonymous telephone calls, to be a child herself who was being abused. It took some time to track her down and several contacts before being able to reach a preliminary assessment.

four cases was of a very serious nature) may account for this. These cases were not ones which aroused a great deal of disagreement between professionals. For the most part sexual abuse was the sole reason for professional involvement in these cases.

Sorting Out Disagreements between Agencies

This was not the main function of any conference. However, disagreements over the handling of investigations and plans for future involvement formed a significant part of 13 conferences. Previous research has pointed to a surprising lack of expressed conflict in child protection conferences (Corby 1987; Farmer and Owen 1995). It may be that sexual abuse cases pose more problems because of the nature of the subject matter and the greater pressure since Cleveland to develop joint investigations. The main disputes between agencies arose, first, over the way in which investigations were carried out and, second, over the extent to which it was felt that social workers should remain involved with cases in a supportive/monitoring capacity.

Interprofessional disputes about the way in which investigations were handled were raised at six conferences. These disputes were between the police and social workers in five cases. Social services department social workers had two main complaints against the police: that they conducted some interviews of children without involving them and that delays in interviewing alleged abusers prevented them from becoming involved with families at the crucial early stages. In one case police were critical of social workers for not involving them or medical personnel in an investigation. In the sixth of these cases, the dispute was between health workers and social workers about delays in an investigation which led to a great deal of pressure being placed by the family on the health visitors (A5.2).

Intra-social work disputes surfaced at conferences in three cases. In one case, which was being transferred from one authority to another, the receiving authority was critical of the previous handling of the case (A2.3). One conference was dominated by a prolonged dispute between the social workers and local authority solicitors about the need or otherwise for care proceedings (A6.5). In the third case, the chair of the conference was critical of social workers for the lack of follow-up of physical abuse allegations made previously (A1.3).

There was disagreement between social workers and other agencies (mainly the police) over decisions reached at four conferences – in all these cases it was felt that more ongoing support and monitoring of families was needed than was being proposed by social services department social workers. This was particularly true with regard to families that had multiple problems and be wise. They wished to maintain their focus on the sexual abuse that had prompted the allegation rather than to become involved in more general family problems. There were variations between authorities in this respect, Seacoast being much more likely than County and, to a lesser extent, City, to maintain ongoing involvement. Other agencies (particularly the police) were horrified by some of the poor material and hygiene standards that they encountered in the course of their sexual abuse investigations and felt families in these cases needed ongoing social work involvement.

Deciding on Future Plans

Formally, deciding on future plans following an initial investigation should be a key function for all conferences. Agreeing on a coordinated plan to prevent the likely or further abuse of children is the prime objective of the child protection conference. However, as has been seen, the timing of some conferences meant that in 15 of the 40 conferences the focus was either on making decisions about carrying out investigations or on tying up loose ends after a period of intervention or surveillance.

In 16 of the remaining 25 cases clear plans were reached and set in motion. In the remaining 9 there was a lack of clarity about future plans. Fourteen of the 16 'clear plan' conferences included registration as part of the outcome. This was true of only 3 of the 9 'unclear plan conferences', suggesting that there is a connection between registration, and the focusing of attention on the purposes of ongoing intervention and on how to achieve those purposes. The defining features of 'clear plan' conferences were an unambiguous statement of the nature of the concerns, a decision on how specifically to reduce those concerns and an agreement about who should be involved in carrying out this work. The following case (A3.1) provides an example of what was judged to have been a 'clear plan'.

A 13-year-old girl alleged that her step-father had asked her to have sexual intercourse with him. Two previous sexual abuse allegations had been made by the girl (against non-family members) which had not led to any effective outcome. The family was part of an extended family that had a history of proven incestuous abuse. The allegation had been made at school, and after a preliminary interview with a social worker and consultation with the police it was decided that the social services department alone should follow up the allegation. At the follow-up interview which was held in the girl's home, she changed her allegation, implicating not her step-father but her uncle, who had until recently been living in the household. The investigating social workers felt that the parents' reaction to their intervention (quiet resistance) was of concern to them and heightened their suspicions. Information provided by health visitors and schoolteachers at the conference gave a picture of a deprived family (there were ten children) with general standards of care that were considered only barely acceptable. This allegation of sexual abuse, together with knowledge of the sexual behaviour of the extended family, provided specific cause for concern. However, the allegation was of non-contact abuse and was not sufficient for the police to become directly involved (and it had also been retracted as far as the step-father was concerned). The conference took place in 1990 and so wardship was a possibility. This was discussed at the conference. However, despite the solicitor at the conference being positive about making a wardship application, the chairman of the conference was adamant about the need to try a voluntary approach first. The decision reached was to register all the children on the grounds of grave professional concern, to appoint two social workers to act as key workers with the family, to liaise closely with the education department to monitor the school progress of all the children, and to undertake some direct work with the 13-year-old who made the allegation. Any lack of cooperation from the parents was to be responded to by renewed consideration of the need for commencing care proceedings. The case was to be reviewed by a full conference in three months.

This case was not at all straightforward in that there were a lot of concerns felt by all the professionals involved, but little tangible evidence of abuse/ neglect and resistance on the part of the family to professional intervention. In the circumstances, the decisions reached at the conference seemed sensible and clear.

Contrast this with the following case which involved an allegation of oral and anal sexual abuse of a 12-year-old boy by his 26-year-old brother-in-law (A1.8). The boy had been joint interviewed by the police and a social worker and had given a clear account of how he had been abused. The brother-in-law had been charged and bailed with conditions to move away from his own family – he had two under school age children of his own. There were, therefore, concerns about their welfare as well. The resulting conference was poorly attended – only social workers and health visitors were present. There were no police officers in attendance (despite the fact that there had been considerable police involvement in the investigation), no probation officer (despite the fact that the alleged abuser was on probation for drug-related offences), and no schoolteacher. No clear decisions were reached at the conference. The children of the alleged abuser were not placed on the register. It was felt that this was unnecessary. However, it was felt that the family needed some ongoing involvement, but it was stated at the conference that the case was not likely to be allocated in the near future because of staff shortages. There was some discussion about referring the 12-year-old to a psychologist, but this was not made a firm recommendation of the conference. The chairperson commented at this point: 'This is going nowhere – absolutely nowhere.' No firm decisions were reached. Future action was left to the social worker who had initially investigated the case.

It is worth noting that the decision-making was made problematic by the absence of key personnel at this conference. This was true of other conferences as well. In fact, it was rare for the police not to be represented at conferences, though key officers (i.e. those involved in the actual investigations) were not always in attendance. The absence of key medical personnel was more of a problem, as was the absence of probation officers in the smaller number of cases where adults were currently known to them.

While there are no guarantees that clear planning decisions reached at conferences will result in better outcomes, the likelihood is that where professionals have agreed to implement a plan of action and feel mandated by it then they will act more positively and this may well have an impact on the families with whom they are working. Farmer and Owen (1995) concluded from their study that there was a link between the clarity of planning at child protection conferences and the outcome of intervention. It may well be that this is only one of the variables that has a positive impact. This issue will be pursued further in the next chapter, which looks at post-conference intervention.

Working with Families up to the Time of the Initial Conference

The period between the making of an allegation and the holding of a conference at which key decisions are made about future intervention can be difficult and traumatic for children, parents and professionals alike. For children, investigations can result in their being removed from home, and guilt and uncertainty about what is likely to happen; for parents, there is likely to be shame and stigma, disbelief and the problems of coming to terms with the allegations. For professionals, there is the lack of certainty about the nature of the allegations, the practicalities of providing protection and help, and of coping with parents, children and the demands of the child protection system, often in a context of limited resources and lack of specialist knowledge or experience in dealing with child protection work.

However, current research is pointing to the fact that the impact of professional intervention in these early stages can have a considerable influence on later outcomes and relationships, particularly in the case of parents (see Farmer 1993; Farmer and Owen 1995). The impression gained from the accounts of social workers in the 40 cases in this study suggests that opportunities for providing supportive help to the various family members were quite restricted. It was noted in the previous chapter that for the most part joint interviews and medical examinations were carried out in a sensitive way and that particular attention was paid to the needs of children in this process. However, working supportively with parents at this stage was far more problematic. Some families resisted all attempts at investigation and so were not amenable to being helped (A1.1, A1.5, A1.6, A2.3, A3.1, A3.2, A4.2, A4.3, A5.1, A6.5, A9.1, A10.1). There was little supportive work that could be done in such cases. Two families refused offers of counselling at this stage (A1.4 and A1.8). For a few cases, supportive work was hampered by the fact that the criminal aspect of child sexual abuse dominated the early stages of intervention. Where alleged abusers were being investigated by the police, there was often no work done with any of the family members prior to the child protection conferences. One case provides a very good example of this – social workers were asked not to visit a family further before the police had a chance to interview the suspected abuser (a time-gap of a week) (A4.3). Some social workers were acutely aware of the fact that parents would be finding this a difficult time. As one put it: 'I couldn't interfere with what the police were doing … that was very difficult because they [the parents] were feeling abandoned as though everybody had forgotten them.' The perceived requirements of the criminal justice system also hampered work with children: in two cases, the social workers said that they were not allowed to do direct work with the children because prosecutions were pending and any attempts at counselling might be perceived as witness coaching. It is interesting that this argument was unquestioningly accepted by social services personnel as an absolute requirement rather than as a factor that should be taken into account in deciding on best course of action. (In one of these cases the child was aged four and the prosecution was not later pursued (A4.4).)

There were, however, some examples of supportive help being offered at this early investigative stage. In the case just referred to (A4.4), where a young child made an allegation of sexual abuse by her father, who was working away from home at the time of the allegation, the male social worker was keenly aware of the mother's difficulties in this situation and worked to support her through it. As he put it, his aim was to:

Try to support the mother in her support of the child … to deal with her feelings about it both in terms of how it affected her relationship with her husband (on personal terms, emotional terms, sexual terms) … it was extremely difficult for her. There were other impacts due to the separation which were financial. She felt she was holding this massive secret from her neighbours. The child could have at any stage started to disclose in the street. This could have severely damaged her standing in the community. For her it's been a dreadful burden.

In a second case, a mother and her child were seen on several occasions before the conference (A1.2). The child (aged 10) had allegedly been sexually abused by her 18-year-old brother. He was an intimidating figure and could not easily be removed from the household. The mother and daughter were placed temporarily in homeless accommodation until the police could interview him. The police did not charge the brother at this stage, which meant that they could not impose bail conditions to keep him away from the house where his mother and sister lived, so they were forced to remain in homeless accommodation. The social worker helped with a brief holiday, schooling and provision of clothes, and encouraged the mother to seek an injunction against her son to remove him from the family home. She clearly developed a close relationship with the mother over this period of time.

Making Children Safe

It was the latter type of case, where children were being protected by being placed in care, that provided the best opportunity for social workers to develop relationships with non-abusing parents and children. Children in 11 cases were protected by residential and foster-care placements, placements in hostels for the homeless and also with relatives. These placements were either required at the time of the allegation or a day or so later when the dust created by the allegation was starting to settle. Place-of-safety orders were used in 5 of these 40 cases. In the other 6 cases, children were accommodated in care or moved in to live with other relatives.[7]

---

7   That making children safe was a key priority of social workers and the police at this period of intervention is borne out by the figures. Apart from the 11 children accommodated away from home, in 10 cases the alleged abusers moved out of the home after the abuse allegation, either through their own volition or as a result of charges being brought against them by the police, resulting in the use of either bail conditions or remands in custody. Children were not living with the alleged abuser at the time of the abuse incident in 13 cases (including 2 of extrafamilial abuse). Children remained living with alleged or suspected abusers in 6 cases. Four of these cases were ones where there was concern because fathers had either been prosecuted in the past or were currently being charged with sexual offences outside the home, but on investigation it was felt that their own children were not at risk from them. In only two cases where allegations of abuse were made were the children left in the same household as the alleged abuser at this early stage (A3.1 and A8.2). In both of these cases the allegations were of a vague and somewhat uncertain nature.

Alleged Abusers

Very little supportive work was done directly with alleged abusers at this stage. The main exceptions were where the alleged abusers were lone fathers (A1.7) or young people themselves (A7.1, A7.3, A7.4). The police were most likely to have direct and exclusive contact with alleged abusers in the course of their responsibilities *vis-à-vis* crime investigation. This lack of involvement on the part of child protection professionals other than the police (except in the case of young abusers) continued in most of the cases throughout the two years following the initial investigations.[8]

Summary

This chapter has reviewed decision-making at child protection conferences and work done with children and families between the response to the initial allegation (i.e. the joint interview in many of the cases) and the holding of the conference itself. The range of case types and the timing of the conferences in relation to the allegations are key factors in the process. Other important factors include the availability of key personnel and, to a lesser extent, the quality of the chairing.

Two factors were of particular concern. The first was the lack of clear decision-making in a significant minority of cases. Many of those cases where the decision reached was not to register seemed to be left with many loose ends. To some degree this was due to resistance on the part of parents and children to further intervention in the light of allegations that were not properly substantiated. In these cases, therefore, these outcomes were more understandable. However, what was of particular concern was the lack of an agreed strategy for monitoring these types of case and for responding to future suspicions/ allegations should they arise, as well as the lack of a follow-up system to check whether needs for help and support had changed.

Second, many of the families who were the subject of child protection conferences because of concerns about sexual abuse had many other problems, including considerable deprivation, generally low standards of parenting care and children with a range of behavioural difficulties. These issues were surprisingly dealt with in only a limited way prior to the sexual abuse allegation, and in many cases this limited response continued after the concerns about sexual abuse had been raised. There was a tendency in many cases to

---

8   This lack of work carried out with offenders is the subject of a research project carried out by Waterhouse, Dobash and Carnie (1994). They point to low levels of therapeutic intervention and a lack of differentiation between offender types in the development of therapeutic responses.

adopt a blinkered approach, with the focus firmly placed on sexual abuse and away from the more general child care issues.

Apart from the joint interviews and medical examinations which were discussed in the previous chapter, the amount of work done with families pre-conference was minimal. The exception to this was in those situations where some residential facility was required, and in these cases children and some non-abusing parents were worked with closely, the need for practical help providing the opportunity for more general supportive work as well. Otherwise there was little direct work, both in those cases where the conference was held very soon after the allegation or in many of the cases where the time-gap was much longer. Many social workers seemed to be aware of the potential needs of the allegedly abused children and, to a lesser extent, of those of non-abusing parents. However, for a variety of reasons – responding to the requirements of police investigations, children (or their parents on their behalf) not wishing to be counselled, outright hostility where alleged abusers and the non-abusing parents were denying that abuse had happened, and to some degree the perception on the part of social workers that their main role was to focus on the protection of the child – the amount of supportive intervention provided for all members of the families concerned in the pre-conference period was very limited. The focus was more on meeting the requirements of the intervention system – by no means a simple task in itself. On the more positive side, steps were taken to ensure that nearly all children were protected from the alleged abuser pending further investigation and decision-making.

CHAPTER 8

Ongoing Work with Families in the Six Months Following the Conference

The material for this chapter was derived largely from interviews with social workers and from reading social work files. As noted in Chapter 3, 28 social workers were interviewed at approximately 6 weeks after the initial child protection conference and 25 at around 6 months after the conferences. Thirty-seven case files were read approximately two years after the conferences were held. Some additional data were gathered from attendance at a small number of review conferences.

Activity in the Six-week Period Following the Conferences
No Further Action Cases
In 7 of the 40 cases, the decision reached at the case conference was that there was no need for further intervention with the families. Three of these cases involved concerns about children who were living in the same households as Schedule 1 offenders. There were no allegations in these cases that the children concerned had been abused by these men. In two other cases involving teenage boys who had been abused and were no longer at risk from the abusers, the cases were closed following offers of counselling being rejected. As mentioned in the summary to the previous chapter, there was no follow-up with regard to the needs of children like these to check whether at a later date they might not be more receptive to, and in need of, some form of counselling. However, the closure of these five cases after the conference seemed reasonable in the circumstances. Agreement to take no further action did not seem to be so reasonable in the remaining two cases.

The first of these involved a case that was discussed at some length in Chapter 7, where concerns were raised about children living in the same household as a man about whom allegations of sexual abuse had been made by children in another household where he had been living previously (A5.2). It was unlikely that the sexual abuse issues could have been pursued much further in this case, but there were many broader pressing reasons to justify some form of ongoing family support – there were concerns about a seven-year-old boy in the family. He was considered to have been demonstrating signs of sexually precocious behaviour from the age of four. He was also thought not to be adequately fed at home, as was said of the other children in the family, who were described at the conference as being thin and of short stature. The mother of these children was considered to be having problems in coping with their care and had become very reliant on her partner, so much so that it was said at the conference that the children would have needed to come into care without his input. The decision not to maintain some involvement in this case seemed anomalous in the light of all this information.[1] As was pointed out in Chapter 7, professionals from agencies other than the social services department were very annoyed at the decision not to provide some form of ongoing support to, and monitoring of, this family.

The second case (A8.3) was discussed in some detail in Chapter 6 – it concerned a mother thought to be making malicious allegations that her ex-husband was abusing their eight-year-old daughter during access visits. There was clear recognition that the girl might be being emotionally harmed by the acrimonious state of her parents' relationship and by being un-necessarily made the subject of several child abuse allegations and invest-igations. Although it was agreed at the conference that the mother needed to be told that there were concerns that she might be emotionally abusing her daughter, this was done by letter and there was no further visiting over this particular incident. Follow-up data over two years showed that there were two more allegations that were also dealt with minimally. It seemed that the professionals (particularly the social workers) in this case were over-focused on

---

1   This is very much the type of case which has prompted the Department of Health (Dartington Social Research Unit 1995) to push for greater support for families and less focus on abuse *per se* except in the more serious cases. This, of course, represents a considerable shift in emphasis from that of the previous policy which, particularly in the case of physical abuse, was encouraging greater child protective specificity. It also assumes that current resources for broader family support are sufficient to meet needs, which is question-able (see Tunstill 1997). Nevertheless, cases of the kind depicted here clearly require family support approaches – my view is that these should be provided alongside more specific child protection functions, which is not always an easy task, but nevertheless one in which the social work profession has long experience (see Sainsbury 1989).

whether sexual abuse had happened or not and, once they were satisfied that it had not, they were less interested in the possibility that the child might be being emotionally abused as a result of the mother's behaviour.

Cases Closed Within Six to Eight Weeks After the Initial Conference

Three cases in which decisions had been reached to maintain contact were closed by the time of the first research interview with the social workers concerned. In two cases the outcome of the conferences had been to carry out a joint interview and to decide on the need for further action afterwards. In the first of these cases there had been concerns because the step-father of three teenage children had been charged with a sexual offence against an eight-year-old boy having previously been investigated in the recent past following other indecent assault convictions (A6.2). In the course of the conference, the schoolteacher of this man's 15-year-old step-daughter reported that this girl had alleged that she had been raped in the past by someone who was now dead. It was decided that the girl should be jointly interviewed by police and social services department personnel. This was duly done. The girl repeated the rape allegation and was referred on to a Rape Crisis centre. No follow-up action was taken.

The second case also involved the need for a joint interview. This was the previously discussed case of the two boys with learning disabilities who were displaying unusual sexual behaviour at school (A7.1). At the joint interview of the 12-year-old, who was seen to be the initiator of the sexual activity, he said that he had had oral sex with two other boys. His parents were seen after the interview. They were told that they should keep a closer check on his television and video watching, which was considered to be a possible source of his behaviour. It was decided that the school should carry out some appropriate sexual behaviour education with the boy. There was no further social work involvement and the case was closed at a review conference held eight weeks after the initial conference.

The remaining case in this category had resulted in registration at the initial conference (neither of the other cases referred to in this section was registered). It involved a 14-year-old girl of Chinese descent who had been in care for a 3-month period prior to the child protection conference (A1.6). During this time she had initially alleged that her father had sexually abused her, but later stated that her abuser was her step-grandfather. There had been a lot of concern about her behaviour which had precipitated her reception into care. She had been truanting from school, taking drugs and alcohol, and staying out late. This behaviour was repeated while she was in care. Concerns were expressed at the conference that it might be difficult to work with this girl and her family. This proved to be the case. The social worker who was made key worker was unable to make contact and the case was closed. This case could be seen as relatively impenetrable.

On Being Persistent

It is a matter of fine judgement as to how persistently to pursue cases where there is a lot of resistance. In cases of physical abuse and neglect, the message that has come from inquiries is that resistance to professional involvement should be viewed as a warning signal that parents may have something to hide (see DoH 1991b; Greenland 1986). In sexual abuse cases the same is almost certainly true – great emphasis is placed by sexual abuse experts on the role of secrecy in enabling such abuse to persist (Furniss 1991). However, possibly because it is not a life-or-death matter and possibly because of the age of the children involved (i.e. they are generally older and seen as more able to voice their concerns, whereas seriously physically abused children tend to be younger and therefore less able to do so), there may be less urgency to press families. The findings of the Cleveland inquiry report (Butler-Sloss 1988), which placed much more emphasis on the rights of children and parents in the process of investigations than previously, have probably had the biggest impact in this respect. Judging from the cases reviewed so far in this chapter, it is clear that a number of the professionals in this study interpreted the Cleveland recommendations as a requirement not to persist where the evidence was uncertain. One consequence of this was that there was a sense of loose ends in several cases where no or little further involvement occurred. Loose ends included a good deal of suspicion that the full truth had not been revealed, resistance to official involvement and rejection of offers of therapeutic input. In some cases the loose ends were of the child protection professionals' own making, that is, they made clear decisions not to follow up cases unless there was a likelihood of taking positive action to tackle sexual abuse issues. In some cases, as has been seen, this approach also led to a lack of response to other areas of child care concerns.[2]

The Remaining Cases

In the remaining 30 cases the activities of social workers in the first six weeks consisted of some combination of the following: more initial joint interviews, further interviewing of children, assessment of the families, support for non-abusing parents, commencing or proceeding further with court action, sorting out care arrangements for children and access for parents, referring cases to other professionals and providing practical help. Of all the professionals involved, social workers provided most of the input to these families, as might be expected given the key worker role allocated to them in the 19 registered cases. The other most prominent professionals at this stage were the police, who were involved in some cases in continuing investigations with a view to criminal prosecutions, and those to whom families were specifically referred for extra help, such as, psychologists and specialist social workers.

INITIAL JOINT INTERVIEWS

Initial joint interviews took place in two cases during this period. In one there had been considerable delay in organizing the interview because the girl involved was a ward of court and judicial permission had to be sought to proceed (A10.1). In the second case the joint interview was held with an allegedly abused child's sibling, who was also alleged to have been abused after the conference (A8.1).

ADDITIONAL INTERVIEWING OF CHILDREN

Further interviewing of children took place in four cases (A5.1, A7.2., A8.1. and A8.2). These interviews were intended both to provide some therapeutic help to the children and also further evidence of abuse. They were the sort of interviews that were disapproved of by the Cleveland Report (Butler-Sloss 1988). The concern nationally about such interviewing was that it put children under pressure and so was in fact neither therapeutic for them nor, because of this, was the material derived from it likely to be permissible as evidence in court. This type of interviewing took place exclusively in Seacoast, mainly in 1990. The children in these four cases were all aged between two and seven, and the social workers involved used general play techniques and more sexual abuse-specific materials, such as story books about abuse and anatomically correct dolls (see Everson and Boat 1994). These children were interviewed weekly or fortnightly on between 3 and 11 occasions. Despite the prolonged nature of the interviewing, the general impression gained was that the social workers involved were child-sensitive and did not apply undue pressure. In one case this was the first time that the social worker had carried out such work, but she was supported and encouraged by a more experienced worker who had received post-professional training in child protection interventions. Efforts were made in all these cases to communicate fully with non-abusing parents, for all of whom this process was understood by the social workers to be stressful.

Despite the care taken, however, the information gained was considered to be useful only for general assessment and therapeutic purposes. In one of the cases (A8.1), there was court involvement in that the parents of the child were going through a divorce hearing. The mother applied to have the father's (the alleged abuser) access suspended pending the outcome of further investigations. The court was ultimately not prepared to accept the social worker's assessment and ordered a report to be completed by a psychologist.[3] Seacoast set up a specialist authority-wide team to carry out work of this kind at the end of 1990. Its emphasis was more on supporting and counselling children rather than seeking evidence. The Memorandum of Good Practice issued in 1992 ensured for certain that the type of interviewing referred to here was no longer acceptable for evidential purposes.

ASSESSING FAMILIES

Most of the formal assessment of families took place before child protection conferences in order that intervention plans could be implemented afterwards. For the most part these assessments were carried out speedily and, therefore, relatively superficially. However, given this, there was surprisingly little formal assessment (or reassessment) of families after the conferences in order to estimate risk. Such assessments were carried out with four families. In one case only the mother was involved. Her husband, who represented the alleged risk to the children, had disappeared. She was seen weekly to assess whether she was aware of the potential risks to her children from him (A4.4). In the second case, both parents were involved. They were seen together weekly. Attempts to see them separately were unsuccessful, which was interpreted by social workers as evidence of resistance to intervention (A3.1). In the third case, the attempts to assess risk by working with the parents were similarly inconclusive (A4.2). The fourth case (A6.6) came nearest to the conventional blueprint for carrying out child protection assessments (DoH 1988).

This lack of formalized assessment should not be interpreted as laxity on the part of social workers. The degree of resistance to outside intervention and focused assessment was considerable in many families, particularly at this early stage of intervention. It was clear from social workers' accounts of the work they were doing with other families that informal assessment of families was going on nearly all the time.

---

3   The distrustful attitude of the courts to social work assessments of child sexual abuse cases in the aftermath of the Cleveland Report is also discussed in a study by Fielding and Conroy (1992), pp.120–122.

PROVIDING SUPPORT

Providing some form of caring support during this period was evident in approximately half of the 30 cases. There was a lot of recognition on the part of social workers that mothers, in particular, needed help at a time when they were vulnerable, either because of what had happened to their child or because they felt betrayed by a partner, or both (see Hooper 1992). Most of the support provided by social workers went to mothers. Such support involved visiting and listening and providing some form of understanding. Occasionally social workers had other motives in providing support, which included gaining trust in the hope of finding out more about the alleged abuse. This was evident in four cases where mothers were either ambivalent about, or resistant to, the idea that their children had been, or were likely to be, abused by their partners. In two cases where this overlap of functions was identified, social workers tried to separate them out by, in one case, introducing a second social worker to focus simply on the mother's needs – she had many problems, including that of caring for a three-year-old child with learning difficulties (A1.5). In the second of these cases, support from a voluntary agency was sought for the same purpose. The social worker who had carried out the initial investigation in the second of these cases (A4.3) was adamant that she would not be allowed to provide support: 'I'm seen as somebody who's part of social services – they see us almost as a brick wall.'

In two cases social workers were dismissive of the mothers' needs for support. They considered that they were not focusing sufficiently on the needs of their children and were putting their own needs first. One of the women was thought to have an alcohol problem. In both these cases it seemed that the social workers were rather punitive in their judgements and inflexible in their thinking about how they could help the family as a whole. Generally, social workers were happier at providing support that was more specifically focused on the sexual abuse issues. There were, however, exceptions. In one case in which two girls alleged serious long-term sexual abuse by their father, who had since left home, the mother's main concern after the initial conference was the behaviour of her 14-year-old son who was beyond control (A1.3). The social worker assessed that he was best doing what the mother required of him in the first place:

> You can only go so far in determining the agenda. When I first went round, I was basically there because her daughter had been abused. She [the mother] had a very different agenda and she had to be listened to. I think the sexual abuse has taken a bit of a back seat. Mother has used me (because she is alone) as someone to talk to ... there are massive other problems ... material and financial.

It has to be stressed that in some cases the possibility of providing any support was very limited. Such cases were those where there was emphatic denial that there was a problem on the part of both non-abusing and alleged abusing parents. There were some cases where it was accepted that the child had been abused, but it was still felt that social work involvement was undesirable – the 'least said sooner mended' approach to the problem.

COURT PROCEEDINGS

Some form of care proceedings was being carried out during this period, with six cases – two wardship applications and four care proceedings (two with a view to securing supervision orders). There was no active resistance to the proposals to these proceedings from parents in five of these cases. At this early stage social workers were mainly being required to write reports for interim hearings. The exception was the case of a 12-year-old girl who was already a ward of court (A2.3). She had made a recent allegation of sexual abuse against her father which had been dealt with by the local authority in whose area the family had previously been living. When the case was transferred it was felt that the father, who had been charged with indecent assault by the police and was on bail pending trial, should not be living in the same household as the child. The receiving authority arranged an emergency wardship hearing at which the case was considered. The court ruled it was in the child's best interests that the father move out. The court proceedings work dominated the early stages of this case.

PROVISION OF CARE

In 11 of the 30 cases children were living in care during this period. Three of these were in care at the time of the allegation – two of these children were moved to other care situations as a result of the sexual abuse allegations. Seven of the remaining eight children were placed in care at the time of the allegation and were still in care six weeks after the child protection conference. Two of these were placed with relatives, and the others were placed in residential homes. The latter were all aged 12 and over. The placement of children in care involved a great deal of social work intervention, the main features of which were providing support for the child in his/her new situation (in particular, emphasizing her/his blamelessness for what had happened), communicating between parents and children, and arranging access. As pointed out in the previous chapter, the practical tasks associated with arranging and organizing care did create opportunities for dealing with some of the more emotional aspects of the situations. Nevertheless, it should also be noted that there was most conflict between parents and social workers in cases involving the need for care placements. Usually the children placed in care were those whose parents or parent did not believe that they had been abused. Many of the mothers in these cases were angry at the consequences of the abuse allegations and not ready at this point to address the issues that the allegations had raised. Their only recourse at this stage, as they saw it, was to scapegoat their children. The following case is a good example of this (A4.2). The step-mother of an 11-year-old boy who alleged that he had been indecently assaulted by his step-brother took the view that he was breaking up the family. She had been abused sexually herself as a child and had never told anyone about it. She felt that that was the way to deal with the matter and that bringing in the authorities was tantamount to treachery. The 11-year-old came into care and the social worker acted as go-between. The step-mother was extremely hostile both to her step-son and the social worker.

INVOLVEMENT OF SPECIALIST RESOURCES

The use of specialist resources was relatively rare at this stage of intervention. It has to be said that in general there were great difficulties in accessing limited resources such as these and, as will be seen, more use was made of them later in the intervention process. Mention of involving specialist resources at this stage was made in six cases. Two girls were referred to survivors groups (both in Seacoast). One had already been attending a group for some time. One girl was referred for counselling. One young offender was referred for treatment to the forensic psychology service. One father was referred to a specialist social worker for adults with disabilities for work on his sexuality. One family was referred to a voluntary agency. At a more general level there was very little interprofessional activity during this period at all – in only one case had a formal meeting of key professionals or core group meeting been held.[4]

---

4   The term 'core group' was first used in draft Working Together guidelines published by the Department of Health in 1986 following the Jasmine Beckford inquiry (London Borough of Brent 1985). In that case there had been concern that after the initial conference key decisions seemed to be taken by social services department personnel only. It was felt that in this case health workers in particular should have continued to be involved so that they could have made a contribution to decision-making. The 1986 guidelines recommended that a key worker be appointed at a child protection conference to organize regular meetings of all involved professionals to ensure that child protection plans were properly implemented and monitored. Research suggests that core groups have functioned in very different ways across the country and that in some areas they have been implemented much more fully than in others (Calder 1990 and 1991).

MATERIAL AND PRACTICAL HELP

Material/practical help for these families was relatively limited. In all, seven families received some form of practical input. In two cases the help took the form of provision of a holiday for the children and non-abusing parents. In one case this was arranged pending the removal of the alleged abuser. In two cases help was offered in securing some form of legal representation – to effect an injunction in one case and a residence order in the other. In one case homeless accommodation was provided. In two cases help was provided in the form of a family aide. Two families were helped with domestic appliances. It was notable that social workers commented on extensive debts and financial problems in two cases but did not see this as an area for them to tackle.

Inactivity

In a small number of cases there was very little activity in this early period of intervention even though the cases were worked with later on. One case which was registered was not initially allocated because no social worker was available to take it on. In another case the key worker was ill for a long period immediately after the conference and there was no one else to take on his work. Two families avoided social work visits throughout this period. As in the pre-conference period, some social workers felt that they were prevented from doing some necessary work by delays in police investigations and advice given to avoid counselling children or parents in cases where criminal court hearings were pending.

Work Done with Families from Six Weeks to Six Months

When social workers were interviewed at six months after the initial child protection conference, a further five cases had been effectively closed, leaving 25 ongoing (62%). Only one of these five cases had been registered initially. This case was closed because the family moved out of the area. The family was one where there had been serious concerns about organized abuse. The children's names were placed on the child protection register of the London borough to which the family moved, but at six months the case was unallocated owing to a shortage of social workers.

Little work was done with the remaining four cases after the first six weeks. In one of these cases (A8.1) there was an allegation by a sibling of the child about whom concerns had initially been raised which led to another investigation and conference. The alleged abuser (the child's father) was living away from the family home and the abuse was alleged to have taken place on an access visit. The social worker involved did some therapeutic assessment work of the type described in the previous section, but the case was closed soon after as there were no concerns about the mother's care and protection of the children, provided access to the father remained suspended. In the second of these cases, the family was proving very difficult to work with and it was not felt that there was any further risk to the 15-year-old girl involved in the original allegation of abuse. It was considered that she was not so much a victim of sexual abuse as of having underage sexual intercourse, a pragmatic but realistic judgement (A10.1). In the third case, the alleged potential abuser had moved off the scene and it was felt that the family, though poor and deprived, did not warrant further help (A6.7). In the final case, involving the family where the social worker focused on the deteriorating behaviour of a 14-year-old boy who had not himself been sexually abused, it was felt somewhat reluctantly that there was no further work that could be done. Two girls in this family had been seriously abused by their father, but their mother felt that she could cope with their needs (A1.3). The social worker expressed concern about the needs of the younger child: 'I suspect that ... in respect of [her] there is little that the department can do ... but we should keep an open mind that in years to come there may be referrals regarding her behaviour and development.'

Overview of Work Done with Cases Open Throughout this Period

Some of the work that was begun in the period straight after the initial conference was further extended; for example, assessment of the family, direct work with children and support for non-abusing parents. Other work commenced during this period, such as preparing children for court and work with perpetrators.

Tables 8.1, 8.2, 8.3 and 8.4 enumerate the range of activities during this period. In general terms, some cases received intensive help and support and others received very little. Much depended on the response of the parents, particularly the non-abusing mothers, as to how much involvement took place.

Table 8.1 Work done with alleged abusers in the period from six weeks to six months after the initial child protection conference

Activity	No. of cases
Assessment	2
Referral to abusers' group	3
Total	5

Table 8.2 Work done with children in the period from six weeks to six months after the initial child protection conference

Activity	No. of cases
Support	3
Monitor	5
Therapeutic work with child	4
Referral to survivors' group	3
Referral for counselling/therapy	3
Self-protection work	4
Help with criminal injuries compensation claim	2
Preparation for court	2
Total	26

Table 8.3 Work done with non-abusing parents in the period from six weeks to six months after the initial child protection conference

Activity	No. of cases
Assessment	2
Support for mother	9
Referral of mother for group work	3
Material help	5
Referral for psychiatric help	1
Total	20

Table 8.4 General work done in the period from six weeks to six months after the initial child protection conference

Activity	No. of cases
Access facilitation	2
Supporting relative foster carers	2
Court work	5
Dealing with further allegations	3
Total	12

Work with Alleged Abusers

The above tables show that the bulk of social work activity in these cases was focused on the children and their mothers. Very little work was done with alleged abusers. Two males were involved in assessment work with social workers. Three males were referred to psychological services for counselling or group work. In only one of these cases, involving a 16-year-old offender in the care of the local authority, was any sustained work carried out. Three factors militated against much meaningful work being done by social workers with alleged male offenders. First, most social workers did not feel that they had the necessary skills to do such work. Second, their focus was on the protection of the child and they considered that working with alleged abusers split their focus and concerns. Third, alleged abusers could not share their problems with social workers anyway because the latter were duty-bound to report criminal offences to the police. Offender work in the current circumstances and prevailing climate is only realistic post-sentencing.

Work with Children

As far as the children were concerned, only a few offers of therapeutic help either in the form of group or individual work were made, and by no means all of these were taken up. Selection for, and allocation of, therapeutic help was a very hit-and-miss affair, depending on the availability of resources, knowledge of them by social workers and openness to them by both children and parents. A social worker who was working with a 16-year-old child in care, who had allegedly abused several younger children, despaired at the lack of systematic follow-up:

> I think if there isn't any great display of stress or severe behavioural problems, then we don't do much. To me, I wonder about that because all we're probably doing is sitting on a time-bomb waiting for it to go off later. Really Sean is getting a lot more treatment than the child that was abused. I'm not saying that one should get more than the other. (A7.3)

Only a few social workers felt skilled enough to do any direct therapeutic work with children themselves. This was evident in only four cases during this period. However, these figures do not take into account some of the more indirect work that arose out of the general contact between professionals and children, particularly in regard to those being cared for by the local authorities. Some social workers felt more comfortable in doing self-protection work with children, which places more focus on educational than emotional issues. While some had attended courses for this kind of work, others were picking it up as they went along: '[We're doing it] through use of certain specific books which deal with control over her own body ... we're looking to do it ourselves ... can't find anyone else to do it.'

This social worker was from City, which was the worst resourced of the three authorities in terms of specialist child sexual abuse workers. County and Seacoast (after 1990) did have specialist resources to take on direct work or to supervise less specialized workers. Nevertheless, even these resources were very stretched and were not always able to meet demand. Very few of the cases in this study had easy access to specialists in sexual abuse work. In some cases good general child care social work practice was adapted to meet the need. Not all social workers felt confident enough to make this leap.

In two cases, children were helped with criminal injuries compensation claims.[5] Only two children were required to give evidence in criminal proceedings. Both were helped to prepare for this during this period by social workers. One of the cases came to court just at the end of the six-month period. The other took just over a year to be finally heard. In both cases the alleged abusers were found not guilty, which resulted in the need for additional inputs to help the child cope with consequent anger and self-doubt.

Work with Mothers

Most social workers felt more comfortable dealing directly with mothers. Providing support for mothers was the most common activity recorded and mentioned by social workers. In some cases, the mothers had themselves been sexually abused as children and the realization that their own children were also being abused left them with feelings of guilt and shame, and rearoused many suppressed feelings from their own experiences (see Hooper (1992) for a fuller account of the experiences of mothers of abused children). Some social workers were very in tune with these feelings and were able to help the mothers, and by so doing help them respond better to the needs of their children. One mother presented with a lot of problems – she gambled and generally came across as a helpless and an ineffective parent. She told the social worker that she had been sexually abused as a child by an extended family member and had never told her mother about it. Presumably she did not trust her to be able to cope with it. The social worker, after initial hesitation, responded positively to her needs:

> We actually made some structured time where she'd come and she knew that was for her to talk about how she saw things ... What is significant is that she was saying, 'I know what my daughter is going through. I know what she's feeling. It happened to me and I feel as if I'm reliving the experiences again.'

This social worker also informed this mother about a female survivors group, but she did not wish to attend. Indeed, most of the few parents and children that were offered group facilities or specialized counselling at this stage were

---

5   Social workers can initiate claims on behalf of children who have been sexually abused without a successful prosecution of the alleged abuser first having been made. Details of the procedures for making applications under the 1990 Criminal Injuries Compensation Act can be found in Denyer (1993), Chapter 9.

unwilling to take up the offer. It may be that many people need more time before they are ready to face up to things more formally. Two key issues arise from this. First, social workers who have already developed relationships with mothers are probably the best persons to provide ongoing counselling where groups (or specialist counselling) are considered unacceptable. However, few of the social workers in this study seemed to have the capacity to commit themselves to extended work with parents. Second, as stressed before, there seemed to be a pressing need for a follow-up system for families where they had initially refused therapeutic interventions, as it is clear that with time needs may well change.[6]

Material/Practical Help

It was pointed out earlier that there was a distinct lack of material help being offered to the sample families at earlier stages of intervention. There was not much change in this respect – only seven of the families who were seen throughout the six-month period following the initial conference received such help according to the social workers' accounts. It is possible that this is an underestimate in that some of the social workers might have provided such help but not raised it in the research interview because they attached little significance to it. Material help identified included the provision of family aides, help with housing, help with clothing and help with household appliances. As stressed previously, some of these families had considerable material problems. It is not clear whether social workers did not address these problems in some cases because they saw them as irrelevant to their main concerns (i.e. the protection of the child from sexual abuse) or because they did not have the resources with which to tackle them. In some cases it did seem that the focus of intervention was too narrow. On the other hand, there was evidence in a small number of cases of social workers being able to combine practical and abuse-specific intervention. In the case referred to above (A1.2), involving the mother who had been sexually abused herself, the social worker not only counselled her and did direct therapeutic work with her ten-year-old daughter, but she represented the family to the income support office and helped sort out housing repairs which were needed as a result of damage

6   While the causal links between child sexual abuse and later mental health and social adjustment are still disputed (see Beitchman *et al.* 1991 and 1992), some studies point to correlations between psychiatric hospitalization and child sexual abuse (see Bagley 1995; Bryer *et al.* 1987; Carmen, Rieker and Mills 1984). It is generally considered (though not proven) that some form of secondary preventive intervention, such as post-abuse counselling, is likely to have some successful prophylactic effects.

created by her son (the alleged abuser) before he had been forced to leave the home. In addition she helped the family make a claim for criminal injuries compensation. This social worker was one of the few that had received some specialist post-qualification training. She could have been expected as a result to be heavily focused just on therapy. In fact the combination of practical help and specialist knowledge of sexual abuse was a powerful one in terms of providing help and assistance.

Foster-care Issues

In two cases children who were allegedly abused were placed with relatives (both grandparents) who eventually became foster-carers. These placements took up a considerable amount of social work time. Such placements, though likely to be more successful than long-term non-relative placements (see Sellick and Thoburn 1996) create many tasks for social workers in the short term, such as sorting out conflicts with natural parents, overseeing the approval process and helping the foster-carers adjust to new demands. One of these cases involved two girls, aged six and seven, who had been living alone with their father after their mother had left home (A1.7). One of the children made serious allegations against the father (which he denied), and as a result both were removed on an emergency order from the home and placed with foster-parents. The grandparents expressed an interest in caring for the children. However, there were two major concerns. First, there were doubts as to whether the grandparents would be sufficiently protective of their grandchildren in that they were considered not to be fully convinced that their son (the alleged abuser) was a risk to them. This raised a very difficult dilemma. In terms of minimal disruption and attachment to the children, the grandparents seemed to be the best option. However, their suitability in terms of continuing child protection was in doubt.[7] Eventually this issue was settled as one of the two children concerned later made further allegations against her father. This resulted in a second police investigation at which the father admitted acts of indecent assault resulting in his later prosecution, thus

---

7   This issue of the capacity of fostering relatives to protect children from potentially abusive parents was highlighted in the case of Tyra Henry (London Borough of Lambeth 1987). Tyra had been made the subject of a care order following the gross physical abuse of her brother by their father, Andrew Neil. She was returned to the care of her mother and grandmother. An assumption was made by the placing social workers that Tyra's grandmother was far more in control of her family than was in fact the case. It was argued by the inquiry that this was partly due to cultural stereotyping of West Indian families, whereby grandmothers are seen as all-powerful figures. Tyra's grandmother in fact proved to have very little authority over her own daughter, Tyra's mother, and was not able to prevent her from returning to live with Andrew Neil, who later killed the child.

convincing the grandparents that the children were indeed at risk from him. The second major complication was that one of the children was not the natural child of the 'father'. The 'grandparents' favoured their natural grandchild and eventually it was decided that it was best that she be placed separately with non-relative foster-parents, despite being very close in age to her sister.

The second case involved two children aged one and two (A5.1). They had the same mother, but different fathers. The older child's father was unknown and the younger child's father, who had been married to the mother, had recently died. There was an allegation that the children had been abused by the mother's new partner. This led to the removal of the children into care. Initially they were looked after by maternal aunts. The paternal grandparents expressed a wish to foster their grandchild, a one-year-old girl. However, there was considerable hostility between the two families which created major problems and considerable work for the social worker involved. Eventually the placement was agreed upon as being in the child's best interests, all other things being considered.

Involvement of Other Professionals

Most of the work during this period seemed to be carried out by social services personnel. As has already been demonstrated, few other specialist services were available and those that were sought were either rejected by the children and families or had long waiting lists, which meant that little work was done in this six-month period. Social workers were not particularly proactive in involving other professionals. Core groups took place (according to the social workers' accounts) in only 4 of the 25 cases. These cases were all in County, which had a long-established policy about core groups and was generally better organized in terms of interprofessional collaboration than either Seacoast or City.

Other Activities

The other main activity that involved professionals during this period was civil court work for social workers. Five court orders were made during this time (one wardship, two care orders and two supervision orders). Sixteen sets of criminal proceedings were also ongoing during this period, but in many cases the outcome was not established until later (see Chapter 9).

Summary

By the end of the six months following the initial conference, 15 of the 40 cases had been closed and 25 were still ongoing. Eight cases resulted in no further action after the conference. It was notable that in five of these cases the conferences were held well after the allegations were first made. A good deal of work had been completed pre-conference and the main function of the conferences in these cases had been to tie up loose ends (see Chapter 7). The main feature of intervention in the 25 cases that did remain open was that the bulk of the work, except for that relating to criminal prosecutions, was carried out by social services personnel. Most of this work was specifically related to the sexual abuse issues. While this might seem to be expected, it was clear that some families had considerable other problems relating to material and social deprivation which were not addressed. With some notable exceptions, it seemed that opportunities were missed to use more general supportive help as a means of assisting with problems arising from the sexual abuse itself. Little specialist help other than that provided by social workers was available to families. For many the time was not right for such assistance anyway. Most of the social work intervention was focused on children and mothers, often separately. There was very little social work input in relation to alleged abusers, whose main involvement was with the police. A whole-family approach was notable by its absence.[8] Arranging care was a major feature of several of the cases, and this work did provide good opportunities in some cases to tackle sexual abuse issues less directly.

---

8   The family dysfunction model of child sexual abuse referred to in Chapter 2 had very little influence on the practice of social workers in this study. Social workers did not explicitly use this theoretical approach to inform either their assessments or their interventions. This could be explained partly by the fact that the focus of this research was on the relatively early stages of intervention – family dysfunctionists, such as Bentovim et al. (1988), have tended to focus on later stages of intervention. It could also be partly explained by the child protectionist focus on giving priority to ensuring the safety of the child.

CHAPTER 9

Two Years on from the Initial Conferences

The files of 37 of the 40 cases were read approximately 2 years after the initial conferences were held. Three could not be traced. There is no guarantee that the material in the files provides a comprehensive record of child protection-focused work during this period. For instance, some families moved away from the area and there was no follow-up of these cases. Nevertheless, the data provide some indicators of which cases persisted and why, and the rates of officially known reabuse.

Cases Closed Within Six Months

None of the 15 cases that were closed within the first 6 months following the initial child protection conferences was open again at the 2-year point (the records for two of these cases were not available). Only three of these cases had been reopened at all during this period. In the case where the mother was thought to be making false allegations that her divorced husband was abusing their eight-year-old daughter on access visits (A8.3), there were two further allegations after the case was closed, neither of which was fully followed up. In the case of the 12-year-old boy with learning difficulties who had been involved in unusual sexual acts at school (A7.1), his 24-year-old sister later alleged that her father had had sexual intercourse with her regularly from when she was aged 14 until she was 21. He was charged and sentenced to six years' imprisonment. There was no lengthy involvement with the family on this occasion. In a third case, the teenage brother of two girls abused by their father came into care for a period, as he was beyond his mother's control (A1.3).

Cases Closed Between Six Months and Two Years

Ten of the 25 cases still open at six months were closed between then and two years after the initial conference. File information was available for eight of these cases. The average time for these cases to be open was 15 months, the range being from 7 to 21 months. In two cases there were further abuse allegations which were investigated but did not result in any significant changes of approach from child protection agencies. In one case the return of an alleged abuser to the home where his sister was living led to her being placed in care for a period of five months (A1.2). Finally, she returned home after he had left again. This was the one case in this group that was purposefully closed. In the rest of the cases, closures left loose ends and mostly came about because no progress was being made.

Cases Open at Two Years

Fifteen of the original 40 cases were still open at two years. Two of these had been closed for part of this time. One involved a 15-year-old girl who was in care for five months after the initial conference following an allegation that her father had indecently assaulted her (A4.3). Nine months later she presented herself as homeless and was placed in bed and breakfast accommodation. Social workers remained involved following her discharge from care eight months later. She went to live with a boyfriend and was due to have a baby. The other case involved a girl of similar age (A1.9). This case was closed 13 months after the original child protection conference and then reopened three months later because the girl was involved in car offences. This resulted in the making of a supervision order and, therefore, in ongoing social work contact. This girl also had a baby at around the same time.

Thirteen of the original 40 cases remained open throughout the whole two-year period. Eleven of these were cases where children's names had been on the register all through this time.

Children in Care

Six of these cases (including the two non-registered cases) involved children who had remained in care throughout the whole of this period, and this fact explains the main reason for the ongoing contact. None of these cases had resulted in placement breakdown, which may be indicative of the success of the placements, but not necessarily of the management of the case as a whole. Two teenage girls who had alleged abuse by their step-father and father respectively were still in children's homes after two years, with only very limited contact with their families (A1.1 and A1.5). In neither case had it been possible to tackle the sexual abuse issues and the situation was one of stalemate.

In another case, a child was in care for a substantial part of the two-year period. This case involved a ten-year-old boy at the time of the initial allegation, who turned out to have multiple problems and seemed to be out of the control of both his mother and the residential staff when he was in care (A5.3). He had been abused extrafamilially. His problems seemed to stem more from lack of adequate parental care – his mother suffered from depression – than from his experience of being sexually abused. Despite being referred for specialist social work help, his behaviour did not improve. He was made the subject of a secure accommodation order at one point in his time in care. At the end of the two-year period, he was placed back at home with his mother because he was less of a behavioural problem there than in residential care. The situation was still a volatile one.

Children at Home still at Risk of Sexual Abuse

There were ongoing concerns that children remained at risk throughout this period in four cases, but the level of concern (or the evidence to substantiate the concern) never reached crisis proportions. In three of these cases the children were thought still to be at risk from the original alleged abuser.

In one of these cases (A6.5), the local authority had secured a supervision order on three children (aged six, four and three at the time of the application) which extended throughout the whole of the two-year period. Almost no progress was made in this case. The man who was alleged to constitute the risk to these children avoided any contact with social workers. The mother of the children told social workers that he was not living with her. The fact that intervention never went beyond the level of conflict and resistance meant that no meaningful work was ever carried out with children in this family. With hindsight, social workers felt that a less direct and less confrontational approach might have achieved more in terms of the children's best interests.

In the second of these cases, the original concerns about sexual abuse had faded. This was the case where the father of two boys aged 12 and 7 had admitted to incest with his sister over a period of many years and was thought to be a danger to his own children (A6.6). This family had multiple problems. Father, mother and children all had learning difficulties (one of the boys severely so). There were poor material standards and worries about the father's style of parenting. The mother was seen as totally dominated by her husband. There were further concerns about the care of the children during the two-year period. The older boy was sexually abused by an uncle and there were suspicions of physical abuse of both boys about 14 months after the initial child protection conference. During this period the father left home to live with another family which prompted a child protection investigation in respect of his risk to the children living there. By the end of the two-year period, the father had gone back to his wife and children. The children remained on the child protection register, with the social worker giving practical and emotional support to the mother.

In the third of these cases, involving the abuse of a four-year-old by her father (A4.4), he had agreed to live separately in order to avoid her being taken into care. Social work input had been focused on supporting the mother and working with her to prevent the father returning home. However, seven months after the initial allegation was made, he did return to the family home without the knowledge of the social workers. This was not discovered until five months later. This discovery prompted a child protection conference at which it was agreed to accept the status quo on the condition that the mother receive counselling, the father see a forensic psychologist and the child be seen regularly by a social worker and health visitor. Regular core group meetings followed. The case was still open and the child's name still on the child protection register two years after the initial conference.

In the fourth case the children concerned (girls aged 11, 14 and 15 at the time of the initial conference) were not seen as still at risk from the original alleged abuser (A2.2). He was already off the scene at the time of the initial investigation and was later convicted of indecent assault, for which he received a 12-month prison sentence. However, there were concerns about general neglect, low standards of parenting and the potential for further exposure to sexual abuse from other men coming into the family. The mother was seen as a poor protector who had colluded in the abuse of her children. Social work involvement continued for the whole of the two-year period, largely at the level of monitoring and with some specific work with the girls around self-protection.

Children at Home Causing General Concern

In the remaining two cases the children were not considered to be at risk of further abuse, but need for ongoing involvement was seen to be in their or their families' best interests. One case involved social workers carrying out ongoing therapeutic/counselling work with a boy whose parents were involved in an incestuous relationship (A9.2). The aim of the intervention was to help him understand and come to terms with his background. In the second case, ongoing support was provided for a girl (aged 13 at the time of the initial child protection conference) who had been allegedly abused by her father and had gone to live with her mother (A5.4). The father was prosecuted and found not guilty a year later. The social worker had helped considerably with preparing this girl for the court hearing. She spent a good deal of time afterwards helping her cope with the mixed range of feelings provoked by the trial outcome. The mother also needed a lot of support as her standards of care were low, despite her being a protective parent. There were also concerns about other children living with the father and his second wife, the latter of whom had an alcohol problem and was alleged to be physically abusive of the children. This case was, therefore, still open at two years, although the name of the allegedly abused girl had been removed from the register 12 months after the initial registration.

Further Allegations Resulting in Child Protection Conferences

There were further allegations of sexual and other forms of abuse or additional concerns about a child's possible exposure to abuse resulting in child protection conferences in 8 of the 40 families over the 2-year period. The nature of these allegations was very varied and did not always relate directly to events that had led to the initial conference. For instance, in three cases (A1.5, A7.1, A8.1) the issue was that siblings of the child about whom there was initial concern had also been previously abused. In three cases (A1.2, A9.2, A4.4) the concern was that the alleged abuser had returned to the household. In only two cases (A2.1,A6.6) were there concerns about another specific incident of abuse to the child who had originally been the subject of concern and investigation. The holding of these additional child protection conferences did not, therefore, greatly affect the direction of intervention in most of these cases. The main outcome of them was to acknowledge changed circumstances and to encourage professionals to monitor situations more closely. As with some of the initial conferences, in a few cases changes in approach had been adopted before the conferences by front-line professionals responding to the immediate needs of the situation and the conferences merely rubber-stamped these decisions. In only one case did a new concern result in a drastic change of direction. This was the case of the ten-year-old girl who had been abused by her older brother (A1.2). His return to the family home after a period of absence led to her removal into care.

Additional Counselling/Therapeutic Work

As was seen in the previous chapter, offers, and certainly take-up, of therapeutic intervention were rare in the first six months after the initial conference.[1] However, some form of therapeutic intervention was proposed for 10 of the 25 cases that were still open after 6 months, suggesting that as involvement continues more needs are identified and followed up. There was, however, little information about the take-up of these offers. Referrals to psychologists were made in four cases. In one case the child referred was the abuser and in two the abused. The fourth child was the 12-year-old boy whose parents had an incestuous relationship (A9.2). In two cases, individual counselling was offered (in one case for an abused girl and in another for the mother of an abused child). Two mothers were offered non-abusing parents' groups and one girl a survivors' group. Self-protection work was carried out in three cases.

Prosecution of Offenders

Prosecutions took place in 16 of the 40 cases, a figure which emphasizes that the study cases were at the more severe end of the child sexual abuse spectrum. Ten were found guilty and five not guilty. In one case there was no record of the outcome. Only two of the children in the study sample were required to give evidence in court, and in both cases their alleged abusers were found not guilty. Two children were intending to give evidence and then changed their minds at the last minute. All those who were found guilty admitted the offences with which they were ultimately charged.

Summary

The 2-year follow-up (using documentary information only) shows that 15 (just over a third) of all the cases in the study sample were closed within 6 months of the initial child protection conference and remained closed. In most of these cases, children were considered to be protected because the alleged abuser or the person deemed to be putting them at risk was no longer on the scene. Only three of these cases were re-referred and the documentary

---

1   This lack of use of therapeutic services has been noted throughout. It is attributable to several causes – the lack of availability of such resources, the reluctance of abused children and their families to use such services, particularly soon after the making of the allegation, and the lack of follow-up to cases to check whether needs and openness to counselling and other forms of therapeutic intervention have changed over time. This lack of use of therapeutic services by children who have been sexually abused and their families is also noted by Dempster and Roberts (1991). They report that of 451 children with a known history of sexual abuse in Dundee, only 41 were referred for treatment.

information about these re-referrals did not suggest that the children had been subject to serious additional risk.

Ten cases (a quarter of the total sample) were closed between six months and two years. Most of these cases raised ongoing concerns, but were closed because there was a lack of progress and it was felt that continuing involvement was non-productive.

Just over a third of all cases (15) remained open throughout the 2 years. Over half of these (8) involved children being in care either for the whole of this period or for a part of it. In four of the remaining families children were considered to be at continued risk. It seemed that social workers were still involved with all but one of these families because they were less resistant to social work intervention than were some of the cases which had been closed.

As far as the records show, the rate of actual reabuse in these cases was very low – 2 out of 40 cases, though it should be remembered that actual abuse was not the concern of all the initial child protection conferences. The prosecution rate was also very high – in over a third of the cases. Therapeutic and supportive input was not at a particularly high level. However, the longer a case was open, the more likely it seemed that such services were to be offered.

The overall impression gained of the impact of intervention over two years was that social work and other professional involvement had had some impact on child sexual abuse. In some cases children were definitely protected from further abuse. In other cases, children were not necessarily protected, but families had been made aware of the likely consequences if further abuse should come to light. A fuller evaluation of social work practice and the lessons for practice to be learned from this study are the subject of the next chapter.

CHAPTER 10

Social Work Practice and Child Sexual Abuse

The Problems of Evaluation

Who Decides What is Effective?

Evaluation of the effectiveness of social work practice in general is a problematic and multi-faceted exercise (see Cheetham *et al.* 1992). There are many different views of what constitutes successful social work intervention – those of politicians (often reflecting the general public view), social work managers, social work practitioners, and service users and their relatives. If we apply this thinking to child protection practice we can see that this is particularly true. Politicians expect that welfare professionals should be able to protect children in their own families without being overintrusive. Social work managers require a quick and efficient throughput of cases with a minimum of mistakes being made. Front-line social workers, on the other hand, tend to judge their interventions in a more qualitative way and take the view that meaningful change within families requires in-depth intervention and, in turn, sufficient time to achieve this. Parents tend to judge interventions (and the success of them) by the way in which they are responded to – in particular they seem to value being treated with openness and respect and being offered support. Older children feel that they need to be believed, but that they should at the same time have some control over what will happen in the future.[1]

---

[1] The social work profession seems to have had a love–hate relationship with the issues of effectiveness. There have been those who have argued that proving effectiveness is the key to gaining and maintaining professional status (Fischer 1973; Sheldon 1986). Others have questioned whether it is possible to evaluate outcomes of social work intervention at all, given the nature of the social work task and the context within which it is carried out (Raynor 1984). Clearly, the social work profession is not alone in finding the issue of effectiveness such a difficult problem to deal with. Current controversies over failing schools and poor teachers are a case in point. Increasingly, effectiveness is being interpreted as a

Satisfying this range of needs is highly problematic. As was depicted in Chapter 2, at different times in the last 50 years of child protection work, different philosophies and approaches have been in the ascendancy, thus determining what kind of intervention has been seen as successful or otherwise. Trying to keep children in their own families was the approach that characterized the work of social welfare agencies between 1948 and 1970. This was replaced by a much more 'child protection first' policy from the 1970s until 1990. The current philosophy is to give more attention to family support needs without overlooking those of child protection. As has been seen, this approach has been supported by research sponsored by the Department of Health (Dartington Social Research Unit 1995). What is very evident from this research is the considerable attention placed on the views of parents (and of children) at the receiving end of child protection investigations. This was a topic that was virtually unresearched in the 1980s and while in many ways this is a welcome shift in focus, the result has been to alter the indicators of successful intervention.

Difficulties in Using Official Statistics

Another approach to evaluating the effectiveness of child protection is a more hard-headed statistically based outcome-focused one, which is less concerned with the viewpoints of the various actors in the process and more with the key question: does child protection intervention protect children from further abuse? The difficulty with this approach is the unreliability of the statistics and the secretive nature of child abuse. Work by Pritchard (1992) using mortality statistics to show that child protection interventions have been successful in reducing the numbers of child deaths has been severely criticized on a number of points (see Macdonald 1995). The main issues are, first, the fact that the official numbers of child deaths by murder or manslaughter are very small and can vary considerably from year to year, thus making it difficult to establish trends, and, second, the fact that we do not know how many of the deaths in these categories are cases of intrafamilial child abuse. A clear, although distressing, example of the instability and vagueness of these statistics arises from the Dunblane killings, where 16 children were killed in one incident by a stranger. A third factor to be considered is that many intrafamilial child abuse deaths may be recorded as accidental. For instance, in both Britain and the USA (Lundstrom and Sharpe 1991; Meadow 1997) it has been controversially

managerial issue, that is, it is seen as synonymous with the achievement of organizational goals.

argued that a significant number of sudden-infant-death syndrome fatalities may be a result of child abuse.

These difficulties are exacerbated when one considers child sexual abuse, a particularly secretive form of child abuse. The only hard measures of success might be a rise in the numbers of prosecutions of child sexual abusers or in the number of registrations of children for sexual abuse (which indeed happened in the 1980s). However, such trends, if identified, might still only be indicative of greater awareness and propensity to pursue such abuse, and not of increased effectiveness in terms of outcome.

Reabuse as an Effectiveness Measure

Another more hard-headed approach is to try and evaluate reabuse after intervention. Some studies have used reabuse rates after two years to try and estimate effectiveness. Dale *et al.* (1986) used such a measure, as did Corby (1987). More recently, Gibbons *et al.* (1995) have used a similar measure. While such rates might have some significance, it should be noted that there are several flaws in such an approach. First, reliance is placed on reabuse being reported, and yet there is no guarantee that all further abuse will come to light. Second, the time-limit of two years is an arbitrary one, usually determined by the practical limitations placed on research by funding. A better measure would be to carry out studies that incorporated a much longer time-span. Third, it is important to be very precise about definitions of reabuse. Is any reabuse significant regardless of its seriousness? Fourth, whether reabuse occurs or not, it is still likely to be hard to demonstrate that there is a link between this and child protection intervention. Again, it should be stressed that the very nature of child sexual abuse, with its associated shame, stigma and secrecy, renders the likelihood of reabuse coming readily to light less probable than in the case of other forms of abuse.

In the evaluation that follows, therefore, it should be noted that there is no particular focus on reabuse (the low levels of officially known reabuse in this study have already been commented upon in the previous chapter). It should also be noted that information is derived mainly from the front-line professional viewpoint and from some direct observation. The main concerns of the evaluation are as follows:

1. Did the work with families seem to be carried out sensitively and openly?

2. Were children adequately protected?

3. Was sufficient attention paid to the general needs of families?

4. Were children and parents helped with their problems in the process of intervention?

Working with Families: Openness and Sensitivity

Corby (1987), writing about general child abuse intervention in the 1980s, found that much work was done in an indirect way without parents fully understanding the concerns of the social workers (and some not even knowing that their children's names were placed on at risk registers). This degree of 'indirectness' was generally not found in this research, though it must be pointed out that the views of the parents themselves were not directly sought, and it could be that social workers felt they were more aware of the reasons for their involvement than was in fact the case. Notwithstanding this, there was generally an emphasis at conferences and in the case records on a direct approach in all but the relatively small number of cases which will be discussed below. This open approach was adopted despite the fact that in terms of the 'participation' movement these were early days so that, for instance, the mechanisms for attendance at child protection conferences were still in their infancy and relatively unused compared with current practice.

In four cases (see Chapter 6 for a fuller account), there was a lack of openness about the cause for concern. In these cases the indirect approach seemed not only to be ethically unjustifiable, but in practical terms it made intervention more difficult. There was still some belief that to be direct about a concern of child sexual abuse might give a parent the opportunity to cover his tracks and prevent further professional intervention. This occurred in one case (A3.1) where a 13-year-old girl alleged at school that her father had made sexual advances to her. The social workers who were called to the school interviewed the girl. She became upset when she was told that her parents would have to be seen. She asked that the social workers not visit her home until the next day, by which time she would have had a chance to tell them what had happened at school. They agreed to do this. When they visited, the girl changed her story, alleging abuse by her uncle. The social workers felt that they would have gained more information by a less direct, more strategic approach.

To some extent the role of the police in carrying out their inquiries hampered openness with a small number of families. In these cases the police wanted to surprise the alleged abuser. There are clearly conflicting aims and priorities in cases such as these. To some degree these issues have been glossed over by the Cleveland findings and those of the current Department of Health research (Dartington Social Research Unit 1995). As will be discussed further in the next chapter on policy, the treatment of intrafamilial child sexual abuse as a criminal offence poses awkward problems for a more participative approach.

Nevertheless, in general terms social workers adopted a straightforward and open approach with the majority of families where investigations took place. These findings are broadly in line with those of Sharland *et al.* (1996). They found that parents were not told about abuse concerns until after their children were seen in 4 cases out of 34. They found that 61 per cent of the families felt the professionals had handled the first contact with them in the right way, 'although only 24 per cent had positive feelings about it' (p.85).

It seems, therefore, that in this respect, child protection professionals have made considerable improvements over the years. Developments in this area are important because, as Farmer and Owen (1995) have pointed out, it is highly likely that the style of intervention at the early stages will have an influence on the way in which families respond later on in their contacts with social workers and others.

Protecting the Children

Again, some reference has already been made in the previous chapter to those children who were thought to be at continued risk. By and large those cases (15) which were closed within 6 months of the initial conferences (mostly not registered) did not come to official attention again. This does not necessarily mean that the children were not subject to, or at risk of, further abuse. In two of these cases (A5.2 and A1.6) (the latter registered) there were concerns that children might still be at risk of sexual abuse, but initial abuse allegations/concerns had not been substantiated and there was little likelihood of being made in the light of this and the attitude of the parents. As it turned out, no further allegations of abuse were made to the authorities in these cases. In another case (A2.1), where there were very serious concerns about the exposure of children to the risk of sexual abuse, the records were transferred to another local authority area following a family move, but the case (despite involving registration) remained initially unallocated because of staff shortages. In a fourth case (A8.3), there was concern that a child might be at risk of emotional abuse because of constant unsubstantiated allegations by her mother that her ex-husband was abusing the child on access visits. This issue was never properly followed up.

Six of the cases closed between six months and two years came to a conclusion in unsatisfactory circumstances, leaving children living with those who were alleged to have abused them or with those who had failed to respond positively when they had made the abuse allegations without matters ever being further resolved. In these cases the efforts of social workers to intervene were resisted and sabotaged. In most of these cases the abuse allegations were not substantiated. In two cases the abuse allegations were withdrawn by the children concerned (A3.1 and A3.2). In two cases there were further abuse allegations which were followed up but again were either not substantiated or blocked by the parents (A7.2 and A8.1).

In four of the cases still open after two years, children were still living with persons who were alleged to have abused them or who had palpably failed to protect them. There were no further allegations in any of these cases.

In all, therefore, it could be said that 14 (35%) of the children who had initially been the subject of conferences were still exposed to some form of risk when cases were closed. It also has to be stressed that social workers in these cases were for the most part aware of these risks. Yet there were only two officially recognized further allegations of abuse, as pointed out in the previous chapter. Thoburn *et al.* (1995) and Gibbons *et al.* (1995) calculated that 70 per cent of children in their studies (which included all forms of abuse) were adequately protected post-intervention.

It is important to note this relatively high level of known risk on the part of social work professionals. It is inevitable that there will be a pool of children known to be at risk of sexual and other forms of abuse within their families unless such children are all taken into care. Politicians and the public need to be aware of this, particularly when they are faced with cases where children are reabused. There is some concern, however, about the fact that a relatively large number of these cases were closed and not subject to ongoing monitoring. In some cases, lack of progress in intervention because of parental resistance was the determining factor, and perhaps in these cases closure decisions were understandable.[2]

However, in one or two cases, decisions to withdraw were linked to resource requirements and the feeling, particularly in County, that active progress was a *sine qua non* of intervention. Another troubling factor was that there was no evidence of a follow-up system in any of the authorities researched to check the circumstances of closed cases at a later date. Further checks were likely to occur only if there were more allegations or risk concerns.

---

2   It is worth reiterating the point made in Chapter 8 that greater persistence has always been expected in cases of physical abuse and neglect – in many such cases public inquiries portrayed social workers being kept at bay by parents who, as it turned out, were concealing the fact that their children were being excessively mistreated. Jasmine Beckford (London Borough of Brent 1985), Kimberley Carlile (London Borough of Greenwich 1987) and Doreen Aston (London Borough of Lewisham 1989) are good examples of this.

The General Needs of Families

As has been demonstrated throughout the presentation of the research findings, many of the families about whom there were allegations or suspicions of sexual abuse were already known to social services departments. Many had a range of material, social and personal problems. Eighteen of the 40 families had a range of problems which in themselves would in all likelihood have prompted social work intervention in more welfare-oriented times. The problems for many of these families included poor living standards and financial difficulties. Some families were experiencing major behavioural problems with their children which were not on the face of it linked to sexual abuse – these included, particularly, school behaviour problems. In three of these families there were concerns about alcohol and drugs. In one family, an older sibling committed suicide after an abuse allegation involving her younger brother. It was never established whether there was a connection. One mother had been hospitalized for depression. In 13 families, at least one of the parents had themselves been abused. Eleven of these had been sexually abused. In five of the families there were children with learning difficulties.[3]

A common theme of the recent Department of Health-sponsored research (see particularly Gibbons *et al.* 1995) has been that social workers intervening in child abuse cases have not looked to the broader needs of families. As Gibbons *et al.*'s research shows, large numbers of families are filtered out of the system without ever receiving any service at all. It is argued that such families are merely screened to see if there is a child protection issue and, if not, are quickly passed over. Gibbons *et al.*'s research is also critical of the level of support offered to families who are made the subject of child protection conferences (about a quarter of the total number of referrals). Only those families whose children were placed on child protection registers (approximately three-fifths of all those conferenced) were likely to receive some form of supportive and therapeutic help, largely of an abuse-focused nature. Those not registered were unlikely to receive any general help at all, despite many experiencing considerable problems and difficulties.

---

3   Westcott (1993) has argued that children with disabilities are more likely than non-disabled children to be abused. Benedict *et al.* (1990), in an American research study, did not find a correlation between abuse and child disability. It is very hard to disentangle the truth of the matter, given the wide variations in definitions of abuse and disability. However, there does seem to be a likelihood that abuse of children with disabilities might not be pursued with as much vigour as abuse of non-disabled children because of the communication problems facing professionals who, by and large, have no particular expertise in working with such children (see Marchant and Page 1992).

In 10 of the 18 families identified as having general problems in this study, little was done to tackle these difficulties. In some cases this was because the demands of the sexual abuse aspects of the cases, such as the need to provide protective care, simply dominated the social workers' time. In these cases the non-abusing parent usually sided with the alleged abuser (hence the need for care provision), and in these circumstances there was usually resistance to social work intervention of a kind which made the notion of providing help in the broader sense highly problematic. The same problem existed where there were suspicions of abuse but the suspected abuser remained in the same household as the child. However, in two of these ten cases (A2.2 and A6.5) it would have been easier to provide more supportive help to the family unit as a whole because the alleged abuser was not living in the household – that this did not happen could be attributed to a blinkered approach on the part of the social workers.

In the remaining cases social workers did provide general help – in two cases they dealt with problems relating to the siblings of the allegedly abused children, and in the others they provided material aid. In two of these cases this help was provided even though there was conflict and disagreement between the social workers and the parents, and continuing concerns about risks to children on the part of social workers.

The difficulty of providing general help and support to families where there are sexual abuse allegations should not be underestimated. Sexual abuse allegations create incredibly powerful tensions between and among family members and intervening professionals. Where there are other family problems as well, it is particularly difficult to tackle both issues except in circumstances where the alleged abuser is no longer a threat to the child because of his removal or departure from the home. In a very small number of cases, more than one social worker was allocated to try and overcome this difficulty. However, such a response was rare, usually because of the resource implications. Providing support can of course help maintain some ongoing contact and indirect surveillance with a family where a child is thought to be at continued risk. On the other hand, as was argued by some of the social workers, this could be seen by the parents as a lack of concern about the sexual abuse aspects.

Meeting the Needs of Abused Children and their Parents

Social workers in this study generally seemed very aware of the needs of children who were alleging, or thought to be at risk of, sexual abuse. For a variety of reasons, however, the help provided was relatively rare and somewhat disjointed. First, few facilities were readily available for children in the areas where the research took place. As seen previously, in Seacoast, social workers did a lot of this work themselves, interviewing children over several weeks in some instances, with the aim of combining therapy provision and the gathering of evidence. Towards the end of the research period, a specialist team took on this type of work more selectively and strategically (i.e. such interviewing was not automatic and referrals for therapeutic counselling were taken at any stage during the intervention). This specialist team, using this more flexible approach, was probably the most consistent and available form of therapeutic help available in all of the authorities studied.

Most social workers felt that they had insufficient time and expertise to offer sustained counselling over a period of weeks. The main alternatives were referrals to forensic psychologists (mainly for young abusers) and to survivors' groups which were run by social workers. However, there were waiting lists for both and the impression gained was that such resources proved useful only to a small number of children. Those cases that remained longest in the system were more likely to be referred for specialist help.

There were, therefore, several barriers to therapeutic help being available to the families in this study. First, social workers generally did not feel that they had the expertise required to do such work. Several of the workers, particularly as far as therapeutic help for children was concerned, were being required to provide such input for the first time. In Seacoast and County there was specialist support for workers from within the respective departments, but there was still a sense of social workers picking it up as they went along. As one social worker who was being asked to carry out some therapeutic sessions with a ten-year-old boy put it: 'I have some anxieties because I haven't done it before, but I think it would be valuable to learn how to do it.'

This lack of expertise was exacerbated by the fact that some of the messages from Cleveland and some of the resulting reactions of others involved in this field, particularly judges and magistrates, acted as further discouragements to social workers and their departments to develop skills in therapeutic work. The problem was made even worse by the fact that little other specialist activity was readily available, and many parents in particular were resistant to the idea of their children talking through their difficulties with a either a social worker or a counsellor or a therapist. This was true of some children too. The latter issue is an important one – clearly therapy should not be forced on people, both for ethical and pragmatic reasons (i.e. it is usually unsuccessful in such circumstances). However, it is also hard to encourage and persuade someone to undertake some form of therapy if there is uncertainty about whether it is available and, if so, about how long it is likely to take before it can be provided.

Of course, specialized therapeutic input is not the only type of help that can be offered, and the impact of providing broader social work support and empathic responses during the course of more general work should not be underestimated. At the very least this can lay down the foundations for more constructive and positive help at a later date. Helping rather than treating has been an intrinsic feature of state social work practice since its inception (Howe 1979). General helping may not be sufficient to meet extreme traumata following abuse, and in such cases it is clear that the availability of direct therapeutic help is an urgent requirement. In many cases, however, a more indirect form of help may well be appropriate. Sustaining this type of help over time is again a problem for statutory social work in the child protection field because of the pressure created by the large number of referrals that require investigative responses – a topic which will be considered in the next chapter.

A final point to be made in this section is the lack of follow-up of cases that were closed where parents or children did not wish to receive some form of help at the time. Again, this lack of follow-up work may have been attributable to resource shortages and case throughput demands. Nevertheless, in terms of preventive work and from what we know of the potential long-term con-sequences of sexual abuse (Beitchman *et al.* 1992), routine follow-up of all substantiated cases of child sexual abuse should be a requirement.

Concluding Comments: Strengths and Weaknesses of Professional Intervention

The main strength of professional intervention (particularly that of social workers) was the conviction that child sexual abuse within the family was something that needed to be tackled and responded to. Child sexual abuse was clearly seen by all the professionals in this study as an extremely important child protection issue. This represents a major advance on what was happening as little as ten years before the time of this study (see the Introduction). Overall, little equivocation was shown by the social workers in this study about the need to listen to children and to take what they had to say seriously and sensitively.

At the same time, however, there was a good deal of realism (mixed with frustration) about the limits of intervention. Social workers in this study were not gung-ho in their approach to child sexual abuse work, and there was little hint of the so-called excesses of Cleveland and the Orkneys. For the most part, social workers accepted the limitations created by evidential requirements. Occasionally they were critical of the police, usually for not pursuing pro-secutions more zealously. Most accepted the view that they were *managing* cases, weighing up the pros and cons of different courses of action in the light of perceived levels of risk. There was some variation between authorities. Seacoast as a whole was more interventionist than the other two authorities and prepared to dig deeper to get to the core of the problem. County's policy was the most pragmatic of the three. If there was insufficient evidence and a lack of cooperation on the part of one or both parents, County's social workers were generally more prepared to close cases. City's practice was more mixed, most probably because there was not a clearly developed philosophy of intervention across all its areas. Social workers were generally less closely managed and directed in their work in this authority, except in regard to the initial investigative process.

The main weaknesses of professional intervention were the lack of specialist knowledge and expertise, and, paradoxically in some cases, a blinkered focus on child sexual abuse to the exclusion of all other issues. The lack of specialist expertise in dealing with problems of child sexual abuse among front-line workers was evident throughout all three areas. Where such expertise existed in other teams or agencies (e.g. other specialist social workers or psychologists) it was not usually readily available. Some social workers were prepared to teach themselves as they went along, but such practice was generally not met with much approval, either from the families themselves or from agencies such as the courts.

Given this situation, it was ironic that in many cases social workers were so focused on the issues of sexual abuse that this overshadowed any other problems that families might have and in several cases led to deadlock in terms of progress. As has already been pointed out, in situations where general deprivation and sexual abuse issues were both present, there was a tendency to overlook the former and to try and tackle the latter. Issues of more general neglect, emotional abuse and moderate physical abuse were in some cases given only limited attention if the initial concern had been about the risk or alleged occurrence of sexual abuse. Social workers who managed in a few cases to combine the general and specific approaches seemed on the whole to have achieved more successful interventions. Those that focused more inflexibly on sexual abuse issues only seemed to miss opportunities to help in a more holistic way. Having said this, it should be stressed that the outcome of intervention was by no means determined totally by the social work approach – the resistance of many families to social work input was a considerable factor in the equation.

CHAPTER 11

Managing Child Sexual Abuse
Policy Issues

The research which has formed the main body of this book raises a whole number of policy issues which urgently need addressing. Some of these issues have been considered in the previous chapter, where the focus was on professional (and particularly social work) practice in this field. This overlap is inevitable, as policy and practice issues are inextricably linked. Nevertheless, in the following sections the focus will be more on the policy level. First, there will be an examination of the weaknesses and strengths of the current child protection system for dealing with child sexual abuse cases. Second, in the light of this discussion and the research findings, there will be consideration of the issues of managing, supervising and training child protection professionals. Finally, there will be some discussion of the broader expectations regarding the control of sexuality in our society, and on how these influence the way in which child protection work is carried out.

The Weaknesses and Strengths of the Child Protection System for Dealing with Cases of Child Sexual Abuse
The Context

The current child protection system has been in place in roughly the same form for over 20 years now. Its formal aim initially was to ensure better communications and cooperation between the various agencies involved in child welfare work in the light of evidence from the Maria Colwell inquiry (DHSS 1974b) that deficiencies in these areas contributed to the circumstances that led to her death. The main features of the child protection system are:

- forums for agencies to share concerns and help develop cooperative and effective policies for responding to and processing child abuse allegations: Area Child Protection Committees

- agreed procedures for responding to allegations of child abuse, usually in the form of procedural manuals or handbooks

- mechanisms for ensuring that front-line workers from different agencies meet to assess and plan intervention for cases where children are alleged to have been abused or are considered to be at risk of abuse: child protection conferences

- child protection registers where the names of children considered to have been abused and/or still to be at risk of abuse are noted and, therefore, particularly targeted for intervention

- a core group and review system whereby those agencies that continue to have involvement with registered cases are expected to meet periodically under the leadership of key workers (usually social services department social workers) and cases are reassessed periodically at meetings chaired by the chairperson of the initial conference.

This system grew and developed at a time when there was concern that social workers in particular needed to toughen their act in terms of protecting children. The social work profession was seen as too preoccupied with the notion of family ties and insufficiently focused on the needs of children to be protected from aggressive and cruel parents.

The key concern of the child protection system from the early 1970s until the mid-1980s was the physical abuse of children and, to a lesser extent, general neglect. As was seen in Chapter 2, sexual abuse issues (in any great numbers) did not come on to the child protection scene until 1985. At this time concerns that social workers were not sufficiently child protective had been fuelled by the findings of the Beckford inquiry (London Borough of Brent 1985). Subsequent policy changes all pointed to the likelihood of even more focus on protecting children from their parents.

Indeed, events at Cleveland (Butler-Sloss 1988) strongly suggested that social workers had learned the lessons of Beckford and the other inquiries all too well. Yet the reaction to child protection intervention there was quite the opposite. It was seen as inflexible and unnecessarily intrusive into family life. Child protection professionals were seen to be overriding parents' rights by failing to provide them with adequate information and to be treating children in an insensitive way in disclosure interviews. There were several reasons for this shift in thinking.

First, sexual abuse was clearly viewed differently from physical abuse. Whereas physical abuse was seen as dangerous and life-threatening, sexual abuse was seen as less immediately harmful and, therefore, requiring more careful and strategic intervention.

A second factor, which to some extent may account for the first, was related to the production of evidence of abuse. Evidence of physical abuse is obtainable via scientific means: X-rays, growth charts and observation (and judgement by medical professionals) of injuries. In some cases evidence is available via the testimony of other adults. Sexual abuse is less easily determined by such means. Much sexual abuse is not likely to provide evidence that doctors can unequivocally attribute to assaults or sexual activity. Apart from the presence of venereal disease in a child there are few relatively clear indicators. The reflex anal dilatation test (pioneered by Hobbs and Wynne (1986) for sexual abuse diagnosis) was largely discredited at Cleveland as evidence in its own right of sexual abuse or activity. In addition, the secretive nature of sexual abuse (see Furniss 1991) renders it unlikely that there will be corroborating evidence of such abuse.

Proving that sexual abuse has occurred, therefore, is more problematic than in the case of physical abuse and neglect. It depends much more on the testimony of the child alone and, in addition, on taking the word of a child against that of an adult. As was seen in Chapter 2, from the early 1980s up to the time of Cleveland, child protection professionals (particularly health personnel and social workers) developed a child-believing philosophy and a range of techniques to help children more easily divulge incidents of sexual abuse. In many ways Cleveland, despite the tenor of its recommendations, put a brake on this child-focused approach. Far from seeing it as sensitive to children's needs, it was seen as overriding them. The later Orkneys inquiry report (Clyde 1992) reinforced the impression that child protection professionals were insensitive and overzealous in their treatment of sexual abuse concerns.

A third factor was the distasteful nature of sexual abuse and the threat that its exposure as a much more widespread phenomenon than previously deemed imaginable posed for social structures such as the family and male hegemony (Campbell 1988).

A fourth factor was that, despite the issues raised by the Beckford (London Borough of Brent 1985), Henry (London Borough of Lambeth 1987) and Carlile (London Borough of Greenwich 1987) inquiries about insufficient vigilance on the part of child protection professionals in dealing with physical abuse, concurrent concerns had been expressed by politicians and the Department of Health about some of the effects of the harder-line approach being adopted by social workers in particular. There were, for instance, concerns about increased use of place-of-safety orders and care proceedings, and the handling of access to children in care (see Parton 1991).

Events in relation to the management of child sexual abuse following Cleveland have been considered in Chapter 2, with particular emphasis on three key policy documents: the 1989 Children Act, the 1991 Working Together guidelines and the 1992 Memorandum of Good Practice. The key messages for child protection professionals in this area of work were as follows:

- the need for close cooperation (particularly as regards social workers and the police)
- the need for strategic approaches to investigations
- the need to involve parents as fully as possible
- the need to take into account the wishes of children.

The effect of these somewhat contradictory developments on the child protection system has been to create a high degree of ambiguity and ambivalence among child protection professionals, parents and children. While the contradictions of protecting children to the least disruption of families have been perennial features of child protective state intervention since its modern inception with the founding of the NSPCC (Ferguson 1990), the particularly problematic nature of sexual abuse, and the increasingly high expectations placed on child protection professionals to get the balance right, have placed considerable strains on a child protection system developed in 1974 primarily to tackle physical abuse.

These strains are exacerbated by the fact that although the child protection system was designed to improve the effectiveness of communication and cooperation between professionals, a less obvious function was to monitor and control the actions of social workers. One effect of this has been to make social workers (and other professionals) more system-dependent and less likely to use discretion – practice has become more 'bureaucratic' (Howe 1992) and more 'defensive' (Harris 1987) as a result.

This context is very important in considering the weaknesses and strengths of the child protection system for dealing with cases of child sexual abuse drawing on the findings of this research.

The Breadth of Child Sexual Abuse

First, a general weakness. The vast range of sexual abuse case types outlined in Chapter 5 provides a major problem for the current child protection system. Very few of the cases in this study pointed to simple or straightforward solutions. Some children were thought to have been abused by more than one family member; in some families there were concerns that more than one child was being abused; some children were thought to have been abused by siblings or acquaintances who were children or young people themselves who in turn may have been abused by others; some children made allegations about events that had just occurred and some about events that had happened well in the past. The permutations seemed endless. By comparison, the issues associated with physical abuse and neglect seem relatively straightforward. Processing this wide range of different case types through the narrow confines of the child protection system was highly problematic. Cases did not easily fit with procedures and processes which were largely designed for investigating single cases of physical abuse and neglect. Another problematic factor was that, as we have seen above, child protection professionals had, because of the recent history of concerns, become very system-reliant. An obvious example of this 'fit' problem was in cases where children were abused by other children or adults living in other families. In such situations, involving two or more families and uncertainties about whether to treat young abusers as victims as well as perpetrators of abuse, child protection professionals, used to one focus of concern, found it hard to cope with the complexity of two or three sets of children being potentially at risk. In most of these cases, attention eventually centred on one family in a rather arbitrary way, given the range of concerns presented.

Investigations

Investigations (and it must be remembered that the cases in this study were the most serious ones of all those referred) were influenced to a large degree by the Cleveland findings and, although most were not carried out in accordance with the Memorandum of Good Practice (Home Office 1992), they tended to replicate subsequent practice in all but the technological niceties of specialist video equipment. Only in Seacoast were there vestiges of the pre-Cleveland disclosure interviews. There was some flexibility in the investigative work, often dictated by resource shortages and the unavailability of personnel. As far as can be judged, despite some interprofessional skirmishes between police and social workers (particularly where they had no prior experience of working with each other), investigations seemed to be sensitively and (for the most part) openly carried out. The views of parents about investigative work in child sexual abuse (see Appendix 2) suggest that, from their point of view, professionals managed this part of the intervention process reasonably well. In the main study, there seemed to be few unnecessary medical examinations of children and, by and large, joint interviews were held in the presence of non-abusing parents. The involvement of the police at the investigative stage seemed to work reasonably well in terms of children and their parents.

However, it should be stressed that, despite investigations being more geared to providing evidence for criminal prosecutions of alleged abusers, the evidence of only two children was actually presented in court hearings and, as was noted in Chapter 9, prosecutions in both these cases proved unsuccessful. There was a relatively high number of successful prosecutions in the study (25%) but, as was also pointed out in Chapter 9, alleged abusers pleaded guilty in all these cases. It may be that the police presence at the investigative stage was influential in securing guilty pleas and there can be little doubt that the involvement of the police emphasized the seriousness of the concerns and gave a degree of security for other professionals and for family members.[1]

Conferences

The utility of child protection conferences for dealing with child sexual abuse cases is variable. As was seen in Chapter 7, conferences in these cases served a variety of functions, but the formally acknowledged function of the conference, that is, to collate assessment material and decide on a protection plan on the basis of this material, was observed in less than half of the conferences, usually where the decision was to register children's names. As Farmer and Owen (1995) have pointed out, child protection conferences serve a variety of other functions which are more geared to the needs of agencies. They ensure that interprofessional cooperation has had the opportunity to have taken place. They act as a check on professionals to ensure that they are not taking undue risks. Professionals use conferences to ensure that they have a remit for their actions. These functions can have two effects. They can lead to defensive practice, that is, no risk-taking at all (the fact that they do not do so to a greater extent is probably due to resource issues), and they can lead to a degree of professional helplessness, that is, social workers and other professionals having decreased discretion and constantly needing to refer back to the conference forum for changes of tack. As has been seen, the timing of conferences is an important factor in determining their function. Some of the conferences held early were no more than strategic planning meetings. Others, held late, were

---

1   Wattam (1997) is far more critical of the post-Cleveland developments. She considers that the demands of the criminal justice system have, via the Memorandum of Good Practice (Home Office 1992), determined the style of child protection investigation in a way that is not necessarily in the best interests of the child. The relatively small numbers of prosecutions resulting from the new system of investigation do not, in her opinion, justify procedures which are inflexible and insensitive to the needs of children and non-abusing parents.

often concerned with tying up loose ends, key decisions having already been made earlier in the process.

While this study could not determine the impact of parental participation at conferences because of the low level of such activity, findings from a study carried out in another local authority area (see Corby *et al.* 1996 and Appendix 2) suggest that child protection conferences do not lend themselves easily to positive involvement of parents because of their size, formality and timing (see also McCallum and Prilleltensky 1996). It seems that there is some possibility of involving non-abusing parents more positively, but very little to be gained from involving allegedly abusing parents. There is a good deal of uncertainty about the benefits of involving children in these forums as well.[2] It can be argued that there is a clear need to rethink the role of child protection conferences in general and in relation to all types of abuse. In the particular case of sexual abuse, the child protection conference seems to be a clumsy tool for assessing, planning and involving parents. A slimmed down forum involving fewer (but key) professionals might be a starting point. Other issues would then need to be considered, such as the type, extent and timing of parent and child participation, the accountability of the key professionals and their relationships with other professionals. What is important is to start from the aims and goals of conferences and to design them around these, rather than simply to add on functions to the original structure which was designed for a narrower purpose (see Walton 1993).

Follow-up Work

Where the child protection system seems, however, to be at its weakest is in relation to follow-up work with all members of families where abuse has occurred. Very few families received any specifically therapeutic follow-up help at all. Some did not want it in the early stages, but there was no systematic follow-up to check their needs once cases were closed. Those cases most likely to receive help at a later stage were those that remained open throughout, usually because they involved children being in care. The lack of follow-up was not due to lack of awareness on the part of social workers, particularly in relation to children. However, there was less general awareness of the needs of non- abusing parents, even though they were often those with whom social

2　The number of children attending child protection conferences is reportedly quite small – see Thoburn *et al.* (1995), pp.9–10. They suggest that local authorities need to adopt specific child-sensitive policies in order to ensure that children attend more conferences and that, when they do, their attendance is meaningful. They point to this beginning to happen in different parts of the country, for example in Avon and Salford.

workers and other key child protection professionals had most contact. A key factor was the lack of availability of appropriate therapeutic facilities. Social services department social workers ran groups in all the study areas (mainly for children, but in one area (City) for non-abusing parents as well), but they were not always available when needed, nor were they always conveniently sited. Psychology facilities suffered from long waiting lists. In the areas studied they were relatively unavailable for children and non-abusing parents.

There was little consideration of the needs of adult abusers. The general feeling among professionals was that they should be separated from the children regarding whom they were seen as risks. Indeed very few social workers, except in the case of young offenders, considered that they had any role at all to play with alleged abusers and very few had any direct contact with them, particularly at the investigative stage – work with alleged abusers was seen very much as the province of the police. There was no evidence of family work done either by social workers or specialist agencies. Therapeutic work (indirect or direct) was largely left to social workers, whose training needs will be discussed in the next section. Much depended on the experience and enthusiasm of individuals for this type of work.

The child protection system simply is not geared to meet the needs of those sexually abused children (and their families) who come right through the system, to say nothing of the needs of those who are filtered out at an earlier stage. It is, as its title attests, essentially a protection system in that, once alerted to risk, its first and primary aim is to establish a means of ensuring a child's future protection. It achieves this wherever possible either by use of law or persuasion with the threat of law, often resulting in separation of the alleged abuser and the abused child by removing one or the other from the household. This is the main strength of the child protection system and, judging from the findings in Chapter 9, it is relatively successful in this respect. However, there is far less emphasis on the effects of abuse (particularly those over the longer term) and on how the abused, abusers and other family members fare. In this respect, the best that could be said of child protection intervention, judging from the areas involved in this study, is that it is patchy. This is a serious shortcoming which could be remedied. The number of children registered annually for sexual abuse is in the region of 6000. There are likely to be another 6000 who are conferenced for sexual abuse but not registered. In addition, there are likely to be many children and adults who would refer themselves were better facilities known to be available. Such numbers justify investment in at least regional facilities. Child protection professionals need to know that they can refer for individual, group and family therapeutic help relatively quickly and with certainty that they will be offered a service. In one of the areas studied such a facility was made available near the end of the research time. However, it has since been closed because of financial cut-backs in local authority funding.

Sexual Abuse as a Health Issue

There are many benefits in putting more emphasis on therapy and health issues in child sexual abuse work, not least that it switches the focus from who did it to how to ameliorate its effects. Of course, the two are linked to some extent in that one way of stopping the abuse is to remove the abuser. However, this is not the sole answer, and, as has been seen, it creates a number of dysfunctions. The Dutch system of responding to child sexual abuse has much to recommend it in that it seems to offer the best of both worlds. The alleged abuser in certain cases has the option of accepting treatment under the supervision of a confidential doctor or of being referred for prosecution. Similar schemes operate in both the USA and Canada (see Bagley and Thurston 1996b, pp.357–358; Macfarlane 1983). While these systems have their imperfections, approaches of this kind at least help break the deadlock whereby an offender will not admit abuse because the only option is prison, a lack of choice which in some cases results in children not seeking help because they do not wish the offender to be prosecuted.

Thus investing more in treatment can have direct and indirect benefits to children who have been sexually abused. Greater emphasis on such treatment and seeing child sexual abuse as a health problem as well as a social problem and a crime could open up possibilities for more flexible and positive interventions without placing children at further risk of reabuse.

Dealing with Neglect and Disadvantage

A final point to be made about the child protection system in its response to sexual abuse allegations is that many of the families referred were disadvantaged and had a range of problems. As has been made clear in earlier chapters, particular focus was placed on tackling issues of sexual abuse. Among child protection professionals, allegations of sexual abuse (and physical abuse) ring alarm bells. They provide something specific and tangible on which to work. General neglect and low standards of care are given lower priority (see Parton 1995; Stevenson 1996). Where child sexual abuse and general poor standards of care coincide, the former tends to be given emphasis. This is clearly a weakness in the way in which the system operates. It is evident that families with these problems need broad-based help as well as specific focus on one aspect of their general problems. These issues were raised in the research carried out for the Department of Health (Dartington Social Research Unit 1995), which is now promoting greater focus on supporting families with multiple problems. This seems to be as important for work with families where children are sexually abused as it is for other types of abuse, as long as family support does not become a substitute for child protection.

Some Strengths

Much in the preceding paragraphs has been critical of the impact of the child protection system on cases of child sexual abuse. Nevertheless, there are strengths in the system as well. Two have already been raised – the process of carrying out initial investigations and the general outcomes of intervention. Having researched general child protection work over the last 15 years, it is also clear to me that there have been overall improvements in the quantity and quality of interprofessional cooperation between all agencies, and that there is a much greater emphasis (for the most part) on openness and explicitness about causes for concern. While it seems to me that the role of the child protection system needs critical reassessment at this stage, these strengths need to be retained and built on.

Managing, Supervising and Training Issues
Management of Child Sexual Abuse Work

In Chapter 2 it was shown that by the mid-1980s responses to child sexual abuse were largely led by the initiatives of front-line workers in social services departments. Some front-line workers, particularly women who were drawing on radical feminist ideas, had far more knowledge about the subject matter than their managers. The main activity of those responsible for the management of these professionals at this time was to react to their expressed needs such as to attend courses where new developments and ideas were being discussed. The post-Cleveland era saw managers placing much more emphasis on taking control of the work to avoid what were seen as the disastrous problems which beset Cleveland, and then Rochdale and the Orkneys. Area Child Protection Committees all devised new procedures based on central government guidelines to deal with sexual abuse cases. These were discussed in some detail in Chapter 2. In the areas researched, the key management role fell to the Area Child Protection Committees and in particular to coordinators of the child protection system employed by the social services departments. These managers, most of whom had background experience of direct child protection work themselves, oiled the wheels of the system, negotiating with other agencies (the police in particular) and ensuring that procedures were followed.

Most of the child protection coordinators chaired child protection conferences. This gave them insight into the way in which interprofessional cooperation was working and they frequently challenged investigations that did not adhere to the guidelines for intervention. In County, child protection coordinators were based in the district offices with the social work teams. This led to closer contact and greater accessibility for social workers to specialist management resources than in the other two districts.

Within the social services departments studied, there was little direct management of workloads. One of the problems that arose as a consequence in all the areas, but particularly in one of the County areas, was that cases were allocated at child protection conferences without reference to line managers within social services departments. This led to cases being neglected because in reality social workers did not have the time to devote to them. In all the areas studied, priority was given to dealing with new referrals rather than to ongoing work. The organization of social work with child sexual abuse cases was not specialized in any way. Child sexual abuse cases were seen as part of general child protection and child care work. There was little allowance for the complexity of such work by social work managers. These factors had an influence on the follow-up work done in those cases held open over longer periods of time, and to some extent account for the lack of consistent informed involvement in these cases, of the kind experienced by many of the parents giving their views in Appendix 2.

Supervising Child Sexual Abuse Workers

The situation with regard to supervision was similar. Supervisors of front-line social workers were general child care team managers. Alongside their social workers they were learning on the job. The general lack of specialism among team leaders created problems for them in managing interventions and meant that social workers did not have the security of discussing cases with experienced supervisors. To some extent the latter need was met by other front-line workers. In one area of County there were two specialist child protection workers. In the other area of County and in one of the Seacoast teams, there were social workers who had attended post-qualifying courses who tended to provide advice and support. However, because of this lack of expertise in supervision, many social workers were tackling child sexual abuse sometimes for the first time themselves and being supported in some cases by team managers who had never dealt directly with such cases themselves. As with the management of child sexual abuse work, such a situation is not acceptable. As constantly emphasized throughout this book, most of the cases in this study were extremely complex and created high degrees of stress among workers.

Training for Child Sexual Abuse Work

The extent of training for child sexual abuse work among the social workers in this study was considered in Chapter 4. Reference has been made above to learning on the job, which is clearly an unacceptable way of proceeding. Some social workers in this study experienced joint training with the police for initial interviews. At the time of the study there was considerable emphasis on this in the wake of Cleveland. In fact the police seemed to take the main role in interviewing, and this has become increasingly the case since the introduction of guidelines in the 1992 Memorandum of Good Practice. Other research has indicated that the role of social work in these interviews has become more one of support for the child and any members of the family who are present (Fielding and Conroy 1992). The main benefit of joint training seems to have been the development of greater understanding by police and social workers of each others' roles and perspectives. In my opinion, this should be the focus of training. Joint interviewing should be one element of this training, not the core. Interprofessional training in child sexual abuse work should be widely established, given the way in which the work is currently tackled, where professionals from different agencies come together usually at a time of crisis. The need for such training would indeed be lessened if there were permanent specialist child protection teams involving all the key professionals truly working together. This was a policy recommendation made by the Kimberley Carlile Report (London Borough of Greenwich 1987) which has never been seriously considered.

Specialist child sexual abuse training with a focus on communicating with children, responding to the needs of non- abusing parents, and working with abusers is also essential if this work is to be done properly. The amount of research material and other writing about child sexual abuse is mountainous and complex (see Corby 1993). The vast majority of the practitioners who were the subject of this research had had little training other than that experienced on their professional qualification courses which, at the time these workers were training, was limited in scope. Two social workers only had carried out systematic additional training in the form of a post-qualifying course. Two others, who were employed as specialist workers, had attended a wide range of short courses. Some others had attended a smaller number of such courses (most had attended none at all). It was noticeable that the work carried out by the more specialized workers was of good quality and that they approached their work with confidence and gave a sense of security to service users and other professionals. Some of the social workers who had attended short courses had been inspired to take on board the new learning. While this was of some benefit, there was a danger, particularly with some of the child-centred material, that it could be applied uncritically, recalling to mind the old adage that a little knowledge is a dangerous thing. This type of approach no doubt contributed to some of the problems experienced in Cleveland and the Orkneys.

At the risk of being boring, I shall reiterate the complexities of child sexual abuse work. Other child protection work is difficult enough given, first, the fine line that has to be taken between protecting children and not undermining families, and, second, the very difficult task of coordinating professionals from different disciplines and with different remits. In addition, child sexual abuse work involves a subject matter that society as a whole is incredibly uneasy with (see below), and that is shrouded in secrecy, ignorance and shame. Such work cries out to be undertaken by experienced and well-trained practitioners from all professions. Finally, it should be stressed that this specialist knowledge needs to be integrated with the general knowledge, values and skills of the various professionals, and not replace it.[3]

Society and the Management of Child Sexual Abuse

The management of child sexual abuse needs to be seen in the context of society and attitudes to sexuality in general. As was seen in Chapter 1, sexuality has, according to Foucault (1979), been subject to state control in different ways in many societies. There have been different views about what sexual acts are acceptable, with whom and at what age in different societies at different times, but essentially despite these shifts it has been recognized that there are boundaries and limits which need to be policed. For many centuries up to the modern era, the Church undertook this responsibility. The nineteenth century saw the medical profession assuming the controlling role. The twentieth century has seen the advent of sex experts from the field of the social sciences on to the scene. Alongside this has been the greater use of criminal law and police intervention to enforce societally approved limits.

---

3   It is important to stress this point. Hudson (1992) strongly argues the case for applying established social work principles to child sexual abuse work: 'Given the mystification of child sexual abuse by many professional experts in the "industry" it is important to insist that the basic principles and skills involved are fairly straightforward and in fact are well understood by many social workers. The idea that only experts should do this work has often undermined the confidence of "ordinary" front-line practitioners most of whom are women' (p.140).

Until the 1980s, the concerns of sex experts and sex controllers were largely with adult sexual issues – homosexuality, prostitution and adult rape. There was very little awareness of, or concern about, controlling sexual behaviour involving adults and children. Now, child sexual abuse has become a central public issue, following Cleveland, the Orkneys and the institutional abuse of children.

The current reaction seems to be one of considerable ambivalence. First, there has been disbelief about claims to the extent of child sexual abuse, particularly with regard to abuse that takes place inside the family. This has led on to the discrediting of the 'controllers' of this 'new' form of abuse: social workers. They are seen as interfering busybodies who, armed with feminist and anti-family theories, are finding abuse where it does not exist. Social workers are (and, according to this study, this perception is true) tackling issues about which they have little expertise and for which they are not properly qualified.

A second response, which has emerged more recently following the persistence of the problem of child abuse, is one of revulsion towards, and demonization of, child sex abusers or 'paedophiles'. Newspapers in some areas have been publishing lists of local 'paedophiles' and their addresses, and in some communities they have been driven out of their homes by local residents. At the time of writing, legislation has been implemented requiring known sex offenders to register their places of residence with the police.

While the concerns of parents living in the vicinity of convicted sex offenders released from custody are understandable, the focus on the paedophile is having some adverse effects. It is detracting attention further from the fact that much child sexual abuse takes place in and around the family. It is also giving the image that all sexual abusers are incorrigible recidivists who are constantly on the lookout for children to abuse. While the most serious offenders may fit this bill, it is unlikely to apply to all offenders, particularly many of those who abuse within the family.[4]

It is in this climate, therefore, that work with intrafamilial sexual abuse has to operate, and it clearly influences practice in dysfunctional ways.

Society clearly has an expectation that such abuse will be controlled in some way or other, and, so far, it has placed lead responsibility for this work on social services department workers in all aspects but investigation (where the police

---

4   Featherstone and Lancaster (1997) make a plea for fuller consideration of issues surrounding male sexual abusers. As they point out, 'Trying to explore and understand…does not mean that we excuse or condone abusive behaviour. Indeed it is a sad reflection of our divided and hostile times that exploring and understanding are increasingly seen as redundant and useless, if not positively dangerous, activities' (p.68).

have gained prominence since Cleveland). However, it seems that the retention of this responsibility is conditional on ensuring that sexual abuse work maintains a low profile and that sexual offending remains within the province of the police and the criminal justice system. This research is hopefully a timely reminder both of the fact that sexual abuse within families continues to be a problem of sizeable proportions and complexity, and of the conditions under which front-line child protection workers operate.

Many of the proposals in this chapter for improving intervention into cases of child sexual abuse have been at the technical level. Emphasis has been placed on improving systems, providing more resources and ensuring better trained and more specialized personnel. Such developments are undoubtedly urgently required.

However, in order for work of this complexity to be successfully carried out, there needs to be some shift in attitudes at the broader societal level – more openness to, and discussion about, sex and sexuality in general, for instance; more tolerance for those who break the rules (without exposing children to greater risk); and more understanding of the problems and difficulties associated with helping families, protecting children and working with abusers. Child protection professionals (particularly social workers) have received a great deal of criticism for the way in which they have tackled child sexual abuse problems. One cannot but help feel that this is as a result of their being involved with an issue which people do not wish to be reminded of. It is almost as if they are also blamed for child sexual abuse happening. This climate is not a healthy one – society needs to rethink some of its views towards child sexual abuse and help create the conditions where it can be managed with better outcomes for all concerned.

The 40 Study Cases by Category

Category 1: Children Abused over Long Periods of Time (9 cases)

Case No.	Area	The abused child	The alleged abuser	The alleged abuse
A1.1	**Seacoast**	**Girl, 14**	**Step-father**	**Indecent assault**

Notes: Father previously convicted of indecent assault, mother disbelieving. Child placed in care. Prosecution – found not guilty. Child still in care at 2 years. Case open.

A1.2	**County**	**Girl, 10 (Christine)**	**Brother**	**Incest**

Notes: Long history of abusive violence. Lone mother supportive of child. No prosecution. Alleged abuser eventually excluded from household after child in care for 5 months. Child at home at 2 years. Case closed.

A1.3	**County**	**Girls, 16 and 11**	**Father**	**Incest**

Notes: 16-year-old abused for long periods, 11-year-old for 12 months. Mother had made the father leave the home when she was told about the abuse. Father jailed. Male sibling placed in care for offending. Case closed at 2 years.

A1.4	**County**	**Boy, 14**	**Father**	**Indecent assault**

Notes: Boy and his friends abused by his father, who videoed the activities. Father jailed. Mother unaware of abuse. No record of involvement at 2 years.

A1.5	**Seacoast**	**Girl, 14**	**Father**	**Indecent assault**

Notes: Father previously convicted of an indecent assault on this girl. Mother disbelieving. Child placed in care. Court case dropped. Child still in care at 2 years.

A1.6	**Seacoast**	**Girl, 14**	**Paternal step-grandfather**	**Indecent assault**

Notes: Girl alleged that abuse had been taking place for 4 years. Parents disbelieving. Child placed in care for a short period. Many behavioural problems. At home with parents at 2 years. Case closed.

A1.7   County   Girls, 7 and 6   Step-father/father   Incest

Notes: Step-father/father living alone with children. Care proceedings following allegations. Children placed initially with grandparents. Father jailed. Children still in care at 2 years.

A1.8   City   Boy, 12   Brother-in-law   Buggery

Notes: Boy alleged that he was abused over a period of 4 years by his brother-in-law, who was not living in the same household but had children of his own. Charged by the police and bailed to live away from his family home. Lone mother believes her son, but no social work involvement. Case closed at 2 years.

A1.9   City   Girl, 15   Step-father   Unlawful sexual intercourse

Notes: Abuse over 6 years. Step-father no longer living in household. Supportive mother. Step-father jailed. Girl involved in criminal offences. Case still open at 2 years.

Category 2: Children Living in Households Where Abuse Seems to be Viewed as Relatively Normal (3 cases)

Case No. Area	The abused child	The alleged abuser	The alleged abuse
A2.1 County	Girls, 7 and 5	Family friend	Unlawful sexual intercourse/ indecent assault

Notes: These children were part of an extended family in which all children were considered to be at risk from different relatives and their friends. The alleged abuser disappeared and had not been traced 2 years later. The girls' family had moved at 2 years and the case was closed.

A2.2 County	Girl, 14 (Frances)	Mother's partner	Unlawful sexual intercourse

Notes: There were suspicions that the two female siblings (15 and 11) in the family had been abused as well. Mother seemed unable to protect them. Her partner was jailed. At 2 years the case was still open.

A2.3 County	Girl, 12	Father	Indecent assault

Notes: The child was a ward of court as a result of previous allegations and her two older sisters had made allegations of abuse as well. The child was placed on a supervision order for 1 year. Charges made against the father were dropped. At 2 years the case was closed.

Category 3: Withdrawn Allegations (2 cases)

Case No. Area		The abused child	The alleged abuser	The alleged abuse

A3.1   Seacoast   Girl, 13   Father   Indecent suggestion

Notes: Allegation that father had offered her sexual intercourse. Later changed her account, alleging that the suggestion was made by her uncle. Previous concerns about child sexual abuse in the extended family. Case closed at 2 years.

A3.2   County   Girl, 13 (Carol)   Father   Indecent assault

Notes: Allegation of abuse relating to incidents several years before. Girl to care. Allegation withdrawn. Supervision order made. Case closed at 2 years.

Category 4: Abuse of Children Discovered at an Early Stage (4 cases)

Case No. Area		The abused child	The alleged abuser	The alleged abuse

A4.1   County   Boy, 13   Uncle   Indecent assault

Notes: Allegation made to parents. Uncle prosecuted. No further involvement. Case closed at 2 years.

A4.2   County   Boy, 11   Step-brother   Indecent assault

Notes: Abuse allegation to parents. Not believed by them. Boy placed in care. Step-brother jailed. Boy eventually returned home. Case closed at 2 years.

A4.3   City   Girl, 15   Father   Indecent assault

Notes: Alleged that father made one sexual assault on her in a public place. Mother disbelieving. Girl to care. Charges against father dropped. Girl returned home after 5 months but later became homeless. Case still open at 2 years.

A4.4   City   Girl, 4 (Bernice)   Father   Indecent assault

Notes: Alleged that father involved her in oral sex. Charges against the father were dropped. Father left family home and returned after 7 months. Case still being monitored at 2 years.

Category 5: Sexual Abuse in Multiply Deprived Families (4 cases)

Case No. Area		The abused child	The alleged abuser	The alleged abuse

A5.1   Seacoast   Boy, 2 and Girl, 1   Mother's partner   Suspected sexual assault

Notes: Concerns raised by relatives about boy's behaviour and things said. Concerns about mother's (and her partner's) drug misuse. Fears about physical abuse and poor parenting. Care orders made. Case still open at 2 years. Children living with relatives.

A5.2   County   Boy, 7   Step-father   Suspicion of abuse

Notes: Complaints from neighbours and sexualized behaviour of the boy at school led to concerns being referred to the social services department. Very deprived family. Decision not to follow up. Case still closed at 2 years.

A5.3   Seacoast   Boy, 9 (Darren)   Stranger   Indecent assault

Notes: Mother suffering from depression and alcohol problems. Boy being looked after by grandmother. Excluded from school and roaming the streets. Into care. Care order. Returned home and still being visited at 2 years.

A5.4   City   Girl, 13   Father   Indecent assault

Notes: Girl living with father and step-mother. Low standards of cleanliness and care. Step-mother has drinking problems. Girl returned to live with he mother who is encouraged to seek residential order. She too lives in materially deprived and hygienically poor conditions. Still being visited at 2 years.

Category 6: Schedule 1 Offenders (7 cases)

Case No. Area		The abused child	The alleged abuser	The alleged abuse

A6.1   County   Girl, 8 and Boy, 6   Uncle and father   Risk of sexual abuse

Notes: Concerns raised about uncle coming to live with family – convicted of physically assaulting a young child. Discovered that father had conviction for an indecent assault many years before. No action taken. Case still closed at 2 years.

A6.2   County   Girls, 17 and 15, Boy, 14   Mother's partner   Risk of sexual abuse

Notes: Partner found guilty of an indecent assault on a boy. Previous convictions as well. Concerns raised at case conference by 15-year-old alleging that she had been raped by someone now dead. No change in family situation. Case closed at 2 years.

A6.3   Seacoast   Girl, 2 and Boy, 1   Father   Risk of sexual abuse

Notes: Concerns about children, who had been made wards of court. Father left family home. Mother not considered to be a good protector but immediate risk eliminated by departure of father. Outcome not known at 2 years.

| A6.4 | County | Girl, 2 | Father | Risk of sexual abuse |

Notes: Lone father with 2-year-old girl. Concerns because of sexual offences in the past. Child also a ward of court from previous concerns. Material needs. Not followed up. Case closed at 2 years.

| A6.5 | City | Boys, 6 and 4, Girl, 3 | Father | Risk of sexual abuse |

Notes: Father recently convicted of sexual assaults on young girls. Lack of progress as parents are uncooperative. Supervision order sought. Case still ongoing at 2 years.

| A6.6 | City | Boys, 12 and 7 (David and Desmond) | Father | Risk of sexual abuse |

Notes: Father cautioned for incest with his sister. Assessment followed by ongoing intervention. Concerns re general standards of care of the boys, both of whom had learning difficulties (one severe). Case still open at 2 years.

| A6.7 | City | Girl, 10 and Boy, 8 | Family friend | Risk of sexual abuse |

Notes: Family had just moved to live with a friend who had a conviction for a sexual offence. Material problems. Mother with health problems. The friend moved out. Case closed at 2 years.

Category 7: Abuse of Children by Other Children (5 cases)

Case No.	Area	The abused child	The alleged abuser	The alleged abuse
A7.1	County	Boy, 15	Schoolfriend (12)	Indecent assault

Notes: Two boys involved in oral sex at school – both with learning difficulties. Not sure whether it was consensual – initiated by 12-year-old. Later allegation by sister of the 12-year-old that she had been abused by her father over a long period. Father jailed. Case closed at 2 years.

| A7.2 | Seacoast | Girl, 6 | Neighbour's child (8) | Indecent assault |

Notes: Alleged abuser aged 8. Denial and no work possible with parents of the 8-year-old boy. Later, a further allegation by a 5-year-old boy in the same neighbourhood. Teenage sister of the alleged abuser committed suicide. Case closed at 2 years.

A7.3   County   Girl, 2 and Boy, 6   16-year-old boy   Indecent assault
                                                           (Sean)

Notes: Initial referral from 2-year-old child of neighbour. Later, 6-year-old child of foster-carer of the alleged abuser alleges abuse. Removal to residential care. Forensic psychologist involved. No record available at 2 years.

A7.4   City   Girl, 14   Boy, 18   Indecent assault

Notes: 14-year-old Down's syndrome girl alleged indecent assault by 18-year-old boy. Both young people living in the same residential home. Investigated but decision to take no action. Case still open at 2 years because of statutory involvement with girl (still in care) and young man (aftercare).

A7.5   City   Boy, 12   Relative of foster   Indecent assault
                                     carer (boy, 14)

Notes: Allegation of abuse by grandson of foster carer. Removal to children's home. Focus on alleged abuser but no progress. Case still open at 2 years because the child alleging the assault was still in care.

Category 8: Abuse on Access Visits (3 cases)

Case No. Area	The abused child	The alleged abuser	The alleged abuse

A8.1   Seacoast   Girl, 3 (Ailsa) and   Father   Indecent assault
                              Boy, 4

Notes: Child alleged to mother that father had sexually assaulted her on access visits. Similar allegation later by 4-year-old male sibling. Long assessment period. Prolonged court hearings. Abuse not proven. Father given supervised access. Case closed at 2 years.

A8.2   Seacoast   Boy, 7 and Girl, 6   Mother's partner   Indecent assault

Notes: Children living with mother and her partner. Allegations made to father on access visits. Allegations not substantiated. Case closed at 2 years.

A8.3   County   Girl, 8   Father   Indecent assault

Notes: Mother made a series of allegations based on her child's physical condition following access to father. Not proven. Concerns re mother's mental health and possible emotional abuse of her child, who did not allege any abuse. Case closed at 2 years.

Category 9: Concerns About an Abused Adult Caring for a Child (2 cases)

Case No. Area	The abused child	The alleged abuser	The alleged abuse

| A9.1 | Seacoast | Girl, 3 | Mother | Emotional abuse |

Notes: Mother made anonymous telephone calls to social workers alleging she had been, and was being, abused. Concerns about her care of her daughter and as to whether the child was at risk from emotional or sexual abuse. Case closed at 2 years.

| A9.2 | Seacoast | Boy, 12 | Grandfather | Concerns re emotional development |

Notes: Case of incest between the mother and maternal grandfather. Concerns about sorting out family issues and helping boy to handle the impact of knowledge about his parentage. Case still being worked with at 2 years.

Category 10: Unlawful Sexual Intercourse (1 case)

Case No. Area		The abused child	The alleged abuser	The alleged abuse
A10.1	Seacoast	Girl, 15	Step-uncle	Unlawful sexual intercourse

Notes: Girl was a ward of court because of concerns about physical ill-treatment within her own immediate family. There had been a previous allegation of sexual abuse. No charges brought – the relationship was seen as consensual. Case closed at 2 years.

APPENDIX 2

View from the Parents

The parents in this study were not followed up and their views were not sought. This was partly because the focus of the study was on the professional perspective, and partly because it was felt that the issues were too sensitive and that parents might feel as if they were being intruded upon if visited by a researcher. A small number of parents were seen at case conferences and reviews, but they did not contribute greatly in these settings and so there was not much material to be used from these observations.

In 1993 the author, along with two colleagues, carried out a piece of research into parental participation at child protection conferences in another local authority area adjacent to those where this research was carried out. Parents were asked if the researchers could sit in at initial conferences and carry out follow-up interviews with them. As a result, 24 four sets of parents were interviewed on two occasions (at 6 weeks and 6 months after the initial child protection conference). Their views about being on the receiving end of child protection interventions have been written up elsewhere (Corby and Millar 1997). In the case of nine of these sets of parents, the concern was about sexual abuse. Interestingly, these parents (most of whom were not the alleged abusers) did not seem to be wary of research involvement and most were only too willing to discuss their experiences. The author interviewed six sets of parents (five on two occasions and one on one occasion) whose children had allegedly been sexually abused. The findings from these interviews are set out below.

General Features of the Six Cases

In five of the six cases there had been definite allegations of intrafamilial sexual abuse against male members of the family. All the victims of the alleged abuse were female and their ages ranged from 3 to 18 at the time of the allegation. In the sixth case there were concerns that an 11-year-old girl might be at risk from her 18-year-old brother, who had learning difficulties and had allegedly sexually assaulted girls on two occasions while in respite care. All the parents interviewed were mothers. In one case the mother and two grandmothers were interviewed. Five of the six cases resulted in registration.

Investigations

Five of the six parents felt that the investigation was warranted (one with hindsight only). Indeed, some had actively sought it. Most felt that the investigations were handled sensitively as far as their children were concerned. One woman was particularly emphatic in her praise of the way in which a policewoman had handled her 13-year-old daughter: 'excellent, absolutely excellent'. Another described the intervention process as 'spot on'. The parent whose son was seen as a risk to her daughter because of his behaviour while in respite care was unhappy about the way in which the initial investigation had been handled. She felt that there was an overreaction. While she agreed that her son had problems that required professional help, she did not consider him a risk to her daughter and felt confident that she could protect her. For her the investigation was unnecessary.

Conferences

Most of the parents felt that the initial child protection conferences were very hard to cope with, despite the fact that they were not the alleged abusers and despite the fact that in the authority where this study was carried out there was good preparation for attendance on offer. One mother, who had initially denied that her husband could have abused her daughter and had allowed him access to the family against the wishes of the police and local authority, and who was, therefore, viewed with some suspicion, found attendance at the initial conference particularly difficult: 'When I walked in that room I felt like dirt. I felt an unfit mother ... I found it distressing; I found it a strain ... I'm glad he [her husband] wasn't there.'

Another mother felt that, despite the preparation, 'it was still a bit of a shock' and said she was 'overwhelmed'. She said that she would not have been able to say anything if her daughter, the alleged victim, aged 13, had been there, which was her right according to the policy of this local authority.

Another mother, whose standards of care for her daughter were in question as well as the risk of sexual abuse, recounted her experiences as follows: 'I felt all the people were against me ... I was talking to cloth ears. They had made up their minds before they went into that room. They were covering themselves. They were not listening.'

This notion of being the object of discussion at conferences rather than a participant was also reflected in the comments of another mother: 'It's all gobbledy gook, isn't it? They're all talking their own kind of language – you just seem to be insignificant. You're just the parent kind of thing. You just sit there and listen to what they're going to do with your family ... they're telling you what you're going to do. If you don't like it you can lump it.'

Work Done After the Conference

There was a general feeling among the parents interviewed that once the conference was over the interest of the child protection professionals reduced considerably. As one parent put it: 'It's as though since all the crisis period was over they've taken a back seat. That's how I feel about them. When everything was going really wrong they were really into it.'

Several other parents reflected on this sharp reduction in involvement with a degree of cynicism and regret because they still felt traumatized by everything that had happened to them beforehand and expected to be better supported. Some were also very concerned about the effect of the alleged abuse on their children and needed some help and reassurance in that area. Visiting in the first six weeks after the conference was limited to one or two visits at the most in all cases. Despite a core group system being in operation, in only one of the five registered cases was such a meeting held within six weeks of the initial conference. The mother of the child who was not registered, partly because she was considered such a strong protectress of her daughter, having responded to the allegations of abuse in a positive and determined manner, was ironically perhaps the most critical of all the mothers about the lack of support she received. She was very angry because the Crown Prosecution Service had decided not to prosecute the father. She obviously had all sorts of mixed feelings regarding her own sense of guilt and responsibility. She focused a lot of this on the social services department: 'The social services department is a bag of rubbish – I haven't even seen them.' She eventually sought out a counsellor who was attached to her general practitioner and saw her once a week for two months. As her comments about the counsellor show, she simply needed someone with whom to talk things through: 'I think she was learning, but she was very, very good. After I had been in I always felt a bit better when I came out. I felt as if someone was listening.'

The perceived lack of direct contact experienced by these mothers continued up to six months after the conference. Two of the families (including that where the child was not registered) had almost no contact at all during this period. Two families had new crises during this period. In one, the mother attempted suicide and was hospitalized. This resulted in her children coming into care. In another family, the mother whose son had been in respite care decided to discharge him, thus precipitating another child protection investigation to assess the degree of risk to her daughter.

In two families there was more ongoing contact because of court proceedings in one case and continued concern about the welfare of the child in the other. Here, the contacts were more frequent, but the parents expressed a great deal of negativity about them. The main concern in these cases for the parents was that they were not being properly listened to. The first of these parents commented about her social worker as follows: 'She's too blatant. You have to be here to see her. You cannot get a word in edgeways, sideways or front ways with her. To me, she's one of these people who's thinking what she's gonna say and she's not listening to what you're saying ... I don't trust her. She tends to twist what you say.'

The second commented about her social worker as follows:

They're not interested. That's how they are. She's got that way where she seems to laugh everything off. She's always got an answer for you.

I still feel now when I go to these meetings [core group], even when I went to court last that I'm just an item. I don't feel like I'm the girl's mother. I'm just this person who's being talked about ... I'm not really being asked what I want. There's plenty of people pow-wowing over the other side of the court and it's all to do with me and the girls. I don't like that side of it at all ... I just sat there and cried. I've even asked if I need go ... I may as well be a court usher – that's the way I feel when I'm there.

Overall, the picture that emerges from this small number of interviews with non-abusing parents is of bitterness about unfinished business and about not being helped with it. There is a lot of anger about social work intervention here, but the anger is not about the fact that the abuse was investigated. Most parents wanted an investigation or were glad with hindsight that it had taken place. The concerns about the investigative process which dominated Cleveland were not raised by these parents. What comes across most obviously is the feeling that intervention is not geared to helping them and their children with the aftermath of the necessary but traumatizing effect of intervention.

As regards the effectiveness of intervention, it should be noted that in all these cases children seemed to be adequately protected by virtue of the fact that they were separated from the alleged abuser.

Summary

These findings have been deliberately separated off from the main body of the study because they are derived from different cases to those that comprise the main sample. While five of the six sets of parents were largely negative about all aspects of social work intervention apart from that of the initial investigation, no claim is made that their views are representative of all parents in this position. To judge from the main study (admittedly using the professionals' perspectives), a higher degree of positive feedback could be expected. Nevertheless, a clear weakness identified in this study has been the absence of coordinated follow-up of cases and a shortage of therapeutic facilities. In this respect, therefore, the feedback from these six parents seems accurately to reflect the situation found in the main study. It should also be noted that the parents in Sharland *et al.*'s study (1996) had similar concerns about the type of support provided for them.

References

Arens, W. (1986) *The Original Sin: Incest and its Meaning*. Oxford: Oxford University Press.

Armstrong, L. (1978) *Kiss Daddy Goodnight*. New York: Dell.

Bacon, H. and Richardson, S. (1991) *Child Sexual Abuse: Whose Problem?: Reflections from Cleveland*. Birmingham: Venture Press.

Bagley, C. (1995) 'The prevalence and mental health sequels of child sexual abuse in a community sample of women aged 18 to 27.' In C. Bagley (ed) *Child Sexual Abuse and Mental Health in Adolescents and Adults: Canadian and British Perspectives*. Aldershot: Avebury.

Bagley, C. and Thurston, W. (1996a) *Understanding and Preventing Child Sexual Abuse: Critical Summaries of 500 Key Studies: Volume 1: Children: Assessment, Social Work and Clinical Issues, and Prevention Education*. Aldershot: Arena/Ashgate.

Bagley, C. and Thurston, W. (1996b) *Understanding and Preventing Child Sexual Abuse: Critical Summaries of 500 Key Studies: Volume 2: Male Victims, Adolescents, Adult Outcomes and Offender Treatment*. Aldershot: Arena/Ashgate.

Baher, E., Hyman, C., Jones, C., Kerr, A. and Mitchell, R. (1976) *At Risk: An Account of the Work of the Battered Child Research Department, NSPCC*. London: Routledge & Kegan Paul.

Behlmer, G. (1982) *Child Abuse and Moral Reform in England 1870–1908*. Stanford, California: Stanford University Press.

Beitchman, J., Zucker, K., Hood, J., DaCosta, G. and Akman, D. (1991) 'A review of the short-term effects of child sexual abuse.' *Child Abuse & Neglect 15*, 4, 537–556.

Beitchman, J., Zucker, K., Hood, J., DaCosta, G., Akman, D. and Cassavia, E. (1992) 'A review of the long-term effects of child sexual abuse.' *Child Abuse & Neglect 16*, 1, 101–118.

Benedict, M., White, R., Wulff, L. and Hall, B. (1990) 'Reported maltreatment in children with multiple disabilities.' *Child Abuse & Neglect 14*, 2, 207–217.

Bentovim, A., Elton, A., Hildebrand, J., Tranter, M. and Vizard, E. (eds) (1988) *Child Sexual Abuse within the Family: Assessment and Treatment: The Work of the Great Ormond Street Team*. London: Wright.

Boswell, J. (1990) *The Kindness of Strangers: The Abandonment of Children in Western Europe from Late Antiquity to the Renaissance*. New York: Vintage Books.

Brady, K. (1979) *Father's Days: A True Story of Incest*. New York: Dell.

Brown, C. (1986) *Child Abuse Parents Speaking*. Bristol: School for Advanced Urban Studies, Bristol University.

Browne, A. and Finkelhor, D. (1986) 'Initial and long-term effects: a review of the research.' In D. Finkelhor and associates (eds) *A Sourcebook on Child Sexual Abuse*. Newbury Park: Sage.

Bryer, J., Nelson, B., Baker Miller, J. and Trol, P. (1987) 'Childhood and physical abuse as factors in adult psychiatric illness.' *American Journal of Psychiatry 144*, 1, 426–430.

Butler-Sloss, Lord Justice E. (1988) *Report of the Inquiry into Child Abuse in Cleveland 1987*. Cmnd 412. London: HMSO.

Calder, M. (1990) 'Child protection core groups: participation not partnership.' *Child Abuse Review 4*, 2, 12–13.

Calder, M. (1991) 'Child protection core groups – beneficial or bureaucratic?' *Child Abuse Review 5*, 2, 26–29.

Campbell, B. (1988) *Unofficial Secrets*. London: Virago Press.

Carmen, E., Rieker, P. and Mills, T. (1984) 'Victims of violence and psychiatric illness.' *American Journal of Psychiatry 141*, 3, 378–383.

Central Statistics Office (1996) *Social Trends 26*. London: HMSO.

Cheetham, J., Fuller, R., Mcivor, G. and Petch, J. (1992) *Evaluating Social Work Effectiveness*. Milton Keynes: Open University Press.

Christopherson, R. (1981) 'Two approaches to the handling of child abuse: a comparison of the English and Dutch systems.' *Child Abuse & Neglect 5*, 4, 435–442.

Cleaver, H. and Freeman, P. (1995) *Parental Perspectives in Cases of Suspected Child Abuse*. London: HMSO.

Clyde, The Lord (1992) *Report of the Inquiry into the Removal of Children from Orkney in February 1991*. HoC. 195. London: HMSO.

Cobley, C. (1995) *Child Abuse and the Law*. London: Cavendish.

Conroy, S., Fielding, N. and Tunstill, J. (1990) *Investigating Child Sexual Abuse: The Study of a Joint Initiative*. London: The Police Foundation.

Cook, K. and Kelly, L. (1997) 'The abduction of credibility: a reply to John Paley.' *British Journal of Social Work 27*, 1, 71–84.

Corby, B. (1987) *Working with Child Abuse*. Milton Keynes: Open University Press.

Corby, B. (1993) *Child Abuse: Towards a Knowledge Base*. Milton Keynes: Open University Press.

Corby, B. (1995) 'Interprofessional cooperation and interagency coordination.' In K. Wilson and A. James (eds) *The Child Protection Handbook*. London: Bailliere-Tindall.

Corby, B. and Millar, M. (1997) 'A parents' view of partnership.' In J. Bates, R. Pugh and N. Thompson (eds) *Protecting Children: Challenges and Change*. Aldershot: Avebury Press.

Corby, B., Millar, M. and Young, L. (1996) 'Parental participation in child protection work: rethinking the rhetoric.' *British Journal of Social Work 26*, 4, 475–492.

Coveney, L., Jackson, M., Jeffries, S., Kaye, L. and Mahoney, P. (1984) *The Sexuality Papers: Male Sexuality and the Control of Women*. London: Hutchinson.

Creighton, S. (1992) *Child Abuse Trends in England & Wales 1988–1990 and an Overview from 1973–1990*. London: NSPCC.

Dale, P., Davies, M., Morrison, T. and Waters, J. (1986) *Dangerous Families: Assessment and Treatment of Child Abuse*. London: Tavistock.

Dartington Social Research Unit (1995) *Child Protection: Messages from Research*. London: HMSO.

Davies, L. (1983) *Sex and the Social Worker*. London: Heinemann.

Davis, G. and Leitenberg, H. (1987) 'Adolescent sex offenders.' *Psychological Bulletin 101*, 3, 417–427.

Decker, H. (1981) 'Freud and Dora: constraints on medical progress.' *Journal of Social History 14*, 3, 445–464.

Decker, H. (1991) *Freud, Dora and Vienna*. New York: The Free Press.

Dempster, H. and Roberts, J. (1991) 'Child sexual abuse research: a methodological quagmire.' *Child Abuse & Neglect 15*, 4, 593–595.

Denyer, R. (1993) *Children and Personal Injury Litigation*. London: Butterworths.

Department of Health (1988) *Protecting Children: A Guide for Social Workers Undertaking a Comprehensive Assessment*. London: HMSO.

Department of Health (1991a) *Working Together under the Children Act 1989: A Guide to Arrangements for Interagency Cooperation for the Protection of Children*. London: HMSO.

Department of Health (1991b) *Child Abuse: A Study of Inquiry Reports 1980–1989*. London: HMSO.

Department of Health and Social Security (1974a) *Non-Accidental Injury to Children*. Letter LASSL (74)13. London: DHSS.

Department of Health and Social Security (1974b) *Report of the Committee of Inquiry into the Care and Supervision Provided in Relation to Maria Colwell*. London: HMSO.

Department of Health and Social Security (1980) *Child Abuse: Central Register Systems*. Letter LASSL (80) 4. London: DHSS.

Department of Health and Social Security (1982) *Child Abuse: A Study of Inquiry Reports 1973–1981*. London: HMSO.

Department of Health and Social Security (1986) *Child Abuse: Working Together: A Draft Guide to Arrangements for Interagency Cooperation for the Protection of Children*. London: HMSO.

Department of Health and Social Security (1988) *Working Together: A Guide to Interagency Cooperation for the Protection of Children from Abuse*. London: HMSO.

Dominelli, L. (1986) 'Father–daughter incest: patriarchy's shameful secret.' *Critical Social Policy 6*, 1, 8–22.

Ellis, H. (1913) *Studies in the Psychology of Sex, Vols 1–6*. Philadelphia: F.A. Davis.

Everson, M. and Boat, B. (1994) 'Putting the anatomical doll controversy in perspective: an examination of the major uses and criticisms of the dolls in child sexual abuse evaluations.' *Child Abuse & Neglect 18*, 2, 113–129.

Fagles, R. (1984) *The Oresteia, Aeschylus*. London: The Folio Society.

Faller, K. (1991) 'Possible explanations for child sexual abuse allegations in divorce.' *American Journal of Orthopsychiatry 61*, 1, 86–91.

Farmer, E. (1993) 'The impact of child protection interventions: the experiences of parents and children.' In L. Waterhouse (ed) *Child Abuse and Child Abusers: Protection and Prevention*. London: Jessica Kingsley.

Farmer, E. and Owen, M. (1995) *Child Protection Practice: Private Risks and Public Remedies – Decision-Making, Intervention and Outcome in Child Protection Work*. London: HMSO.

Featherstone, B. and Lancaster E. (1997) 'Contemplating the unthinkable: men who sexually abuse children.' *Critical Social Policy 17*, 4, 51–68.

Ferguson, H. (1990) 'Rethinking child protection practices: a case for history.' In The Violence Against Children Study Group, *Taking Child Abuse Seriously; Contemporary Issues in Child Protection Theory and Practice*. London: Allen & Unwin.

Ferguson, H. (1996) 'The protection of children in time: child protection and the lives and deaths of children in child abuse cases in socio-historical perspective.' *Child and Family Social Work 1*, 4, 205–217.

Fielding, N. and Conroy, S. (1992) 'Interviewing child victims: police and social work investigations of child sexual abuse.' *Sociology 26*, 1, 103–124.

Finkelhor, D. (1979a) 'What's wrong with sex between adults and children? Ethics and the problem of child sexual abuse.' *American Journal of Orthopsychiatry 49*, 4, 692–697.

Finkelhor, D. (1979b) *Sexually Victimized Children*. New York: The Free Press.

Finkelhor, D. and Baron, L. (1986) 'High-risk children.' In D. Finkelhor and associates (eds) *A Sourcebook on Child Sexual Abuse*. Newbury Park: Sage.

Finkelhor, D. and associates (eds) (1986) *A Sourcebook on Child Sexual Abuse*. Newbury Park: Sage.

Fischer, J. (1973) 'Is casework effective? A review.' *Social Work 18*, 1, 5–21.

Fisher, T. (1997) 'Learning about child protection.' *Social Work Education 16*, 2, 92–112.

Foucault, M. (1979) *The History of Sexuality: An Introduction*. London: Allen Lane.

Foucault, M. (1985) *The Use of Pleasure*. Harmondsworth: Penguin.

Foucault, M. (1986) *The Care of the Self*. Harmondsworth: Penguin.

Fraser, B. (1976) 'The child and his parents: a delicate balance of rights.' In R. Helfer and C. Kempe (eds) *Child Abuse and Neglect: The Family and the Community*. Cambridge, Mass: Ballinger.

Friedrich, W., Grambsch, P., Broughton, P., Kuiper, J. and Beilke, R. (1991) 'Normative sexual behavior in children.' *Pediatrics 88*, 456–464.

Frosh, S. (1988) 'No man's land?: The role of men working with sexually abused children.' *British Journal of Guidance and Counselling 16*, 1, 1–10.

Furniss, T. (1991) *The Multi-Professional Handbook of Child Sexual Abuse: Integrated Management, Therapy and Legal Intervention*. London: Routledge.

Gagnon, J. and Parker, R. (1995) *Conceiving Sexuality: Approaches to Sex Research in the Modern World*. London: Routledge.

Gallagher, B., Hughes, B. and Parker, H. (1996) 'The nature and extent of known cases of organised sexual abuse in England and Wales.' In P. Bibby (ed) *Organised Abuse: The Current Debate.* Aldershot: Arena/Ashgate.

Giaretto, H. (1981) 'A comprehensive child sexual abuse treatment program.' In P. Mrazek and C. Kempe (eds) *Sexually Abused Children and their Families.* Oxford: Pergamon Press.

Gibbons, J., Conroy, S. and Bell, C. (1995) *Operation of Child Protection Registers: A Study of Child Protection Practices in English Local Authorities.* London: HMSO.

Glaser, D. and Frosh, S. (1988) *Child Sexual Abuse.* Basingstoke: Macmillan.

Gomes-Schwartz, B., Horowitz, J. and Cardarelli, A. (1990) *Child Sexual Abuse: The Initial Effects.* Beverly Hills: Sage.

Gordon, L. (1989) *Heroes of their own Lives: The Politics and History of Family Violence, Boston 1880–1960.* London: Virago Press.

Gordon, M. (1989) 'The family environment of sexual abuse: a comparison of natal and step-father abuse.' *Child Abuse & Neglect 13,* 121–130.

Gorham, D. (1978) 'The maiden tribute of Babylon reexamined: child prostitution and the idea of childhood in late-Victorian England.' *Victorian Studies 21,* 3, 54–379.

Greenland, C. (1958) 'Incest.' *British Journal of Delinquency 9a,* 1, 62–65.

Greenland, C. (1986) 'Inquiries into child abuse and neglect (CAN) deaths in the United Kingdom.' *British Journal of Criminology 26,* 164–173.

Groth, A. (1979) *Men Who Rape: A Psychology of the Offender.* New York: Plenum Press.

Groth, A. and Birnbaum, J. (1978) 'Adult sexual orientation and attraction to underage persons.' *Archives of Sexual Behavior 7,* 3, 175–181.

Hall, L. and Lloyd, S. (1993) *Surviving Child Sexual Abuse: A Handbook for Helping Women Challenge their Past.* London: Falmer Press.

Hallett, C. (1989) 'Child abuse inquiries and public policy.' In O. Stevenson (ed) *Child Abuse: Public Policy and Professional Practice.* Hemel Hempstead: Harvester Wheatsheaf.

Hallett, C. and Birchall, E. (1992) *Coordination and Child Protection: A Review of the Literature.* Edinburgh: HMSO.

Hallett, C. and Stevenson, O. (1980) *Child Abuse: Aspects of Interprofessional Cooperation.* London: Allen & Unwin.

Harris, N. (1987) 'Defensive social work.' *British Journal of Social Work 17,* 1, 61–69.

Helfer, R. and Kempe, C. (eds) (1968) *The Battered Child.* Chicago: University of Chicago Press.

Hite, S. (1976) *The Hite Report on Female Sexuality.* London: Macmillan.

Hite, S. (1981) *The Hite Report on Male Sexuality.* London: Macmillan.

Hobbs, C. and Wynne, J. (1986) 'Buggery in childhood – a common syndrome of child abuse.' *The Lancet ii,* 792–796.

Home Office (1988) *The Investigation of Child Sexual Abuse. Circular 52 1988.* London: HMSO.

Home Office (1989) *Report of the Advisory Group on Video Evidence.* London: HMSO.

Home Office (in conjunction with the Department of Health) (1992) *Memorandum of Good Practice on Video Recorded Interviews with Child Witnesses for Criminal Proceedings.* London: HMSO.

Hooper, C.A. (1992) *Mothers Surviving Child Sexual Abuse.* London: Tavistock.

Horne, L., Glasgow, D., Cox, A. and Calam, R. (1991) 'Sexual abuse of children by children.' *Journal of Child Law 3,* 4, 147–151.

House of Commons (1984) *Children in Care: Second Report from the Social Services Committee* (Session 1983). London: HMSO.

Howe, D. (1979) 'Agency function and social work principles.' *British Journal of Social Work 9,* 1, 26–48.

Howe, D. (1992) 'Child abuse and the bureaucratisation of social work.' *Sociological Review 40,* 3, 491–508.

Hudson, A. (1992) 'The child sexual abuse "industry" and gender relations in social work.' In M. Langan and L. Day (eds) *Women, Oppression and Social Work Issues in Anti-Discriminatory Practice.* London: Routledge.

Jorne, P. (1979) 'Treating sexually abused children.' *Child Abuse & Neglect 3*, 1, 285–290.

Kelly, L. and Regan, L. (1990) 'Flawed protection.' *Social Work Today 21*, 32, 13–15.

Kempe, C. (1978) 'Sexual abuse: another hidden pediatric problem.' *Pediatrics 62*, 3, 382–389.

Kempe, C., Silverman, F., Steele, B., Droegemueller, W. and Silver, H. (1962) 'The battered child syndrome.' *Journal of the American Medical Association 181*, 1, 17–24.

Kinsey, A., Pomeroy, W., Martin, C. and Gebhard, P. (1948) *Sexual Behaviour in the Human Male.* Philadelphia: W.B. Saunders & Co.

Kinsey, A., Pomeroy, W., Martin, C. and Gebhard, P. (1953) *Sexual Behaviour in the Human Female.* Philadelphia: W.B. Saunders & Co.

Kirk, G. (1979) *The Bacchae of Euripides.* Cambridge: Cambridge University Press.

LaFontaine, J. (1988) *Child Sexual Abuse: An ESRC Research Briefing.* London: Economic and Social Research Council.

LaFontaine, J. (1990) *Child Sexual Abuse.* Cambridge: Polity Press.

LaFontaine, J. (1994) *The Extent and Nature of Organised and Ritual Abuse: Research Findings.* London: HMSO.

Lewis, A. (1992) 'An overview of research into participation in child protection work.' In J. Thoburn (ed) *Participation in Practice – Involving Families in Child Protection.* Norwich: University of East Anglia Press.

Lewis, A. (1994) *Chairing Child Protection Conferences.* Aldershot: Avebury.

London Borough of Brent (1985) *A Child in Trust: The Report of the Panel of Inquiry into the Circumstances Surrounding the Death of Jasmine Beckford.* London: Brent MB.

London Borough of Greenwich (1987) *A Child in Mind: Protection of Children in a Responsible Society: The Report of the Commission of Inquiry into the Circumstances Surrounding the Death of Kimberley Carlile.* London: Greenwich MB.

London Borough of Lambeth (1987) *Whose Child? The Report of the Panel Appointed to Inquire into the Death of Tyra Henry.* London: Lambeth MB.

London Borough of Lewisham (1989) *The Doreen Aston Report.* London: Lewisham MB.

Lundstrom, M. and Sharpe, R. (1991) 'Getting away with murder.' *Public Welfare 49*, 3, 18–29.

Lyon, C. and DeCruz, P. (1993) *Child Abuse.* 2nd Edition. Bristol: Jordan.

McCallum, S. and Prilleltensky, I. (1996) 'Empowerment in child protection work: values, practice and caveats.' *Children & Society 10*, 1, 40–50.

Macdonald, K. (1995) 'Comparative homicide and the proper aims of social work: a sceptical note.' *British Journal of Social Work 25*, 4, 489–497.

Macfarlane, K. (1983) 'Program consideration in the treatment of offenders.' In J. Geer and I. Stuart (eds) *The Sexual Aggressor: Current Perspectives in Treatment.* New York: Van Nostrand Reinhold.

Macfarlane, K. and Waterman, J. (1986) *The Sexual Abuse of Young Children.* New York: Holt, Rinehart & Winston.

Macleod, M. and Saraga, E. (eds) (1988) 'Family secrets: child sexual abuse today.' *Feminist Review 28*, Spring, 16–55.

Mcnay, L. (1994) *Foucault: A Critical Introduction.* Cambridge: Polity Press.

Marchant, R. and Page, M. (1992) *Bridging the Gap: Child Protection Work with Children with Multiple Disabilities.* London: NSPCC.

Masson, J. (1984) *Freud: The Assault on Truth.* London: Faber & Faber.

Masson, J. (1989) *Against Therapy.* London: Collins.

Masters, W. and Johnson, V. (1966) *The Human Sexual Response.* Boston: Little, Brown & Co.

Masters, W. and Johnson, V. (1970) *Human Sexual Inadequacy.* Boston: Little, Brown & Co.

Meadow, R. (1997) 'Fatal abuse and smothering.' In R. Meadow (ed) *ABC of Child Abuse*. Bristol: BMJ Publishing Group.

Metropolitan Police and London Borough of Bexley (1987) *Child Sexual Abuse: Joint Investigative Programme: Bexley Experiment: Final Report*. London: HMSO.

Miller, A. (1985) *Thou Shalt Not Be Aware*. London: Pluto Press.

Milner, J. (1986) *Social Work and Sexual Problems: A Practical Guide for Social Workers*. Birmingham: PEPAR.

Milner, J.S. (1994) 'Is poverty a key contributor to child maltreatment?' In E. Gambrill and T. Stein *Controversial Issues in Child Welfare*. London: Allyn & Bacon.

Moran-Ellis, J. and Fielding, N. (1996) 'A national survey of the investigation of child sexual abuse.' *British Journal of Social Work 26*, 3, 337–356.

Morrison, T., Erooga, M. and Beckett, R. (eds) (1994) *Sexual Offending against Children: Assessment and Treatment of Male Abusers*. London: Routledge.

Mrazek, P. and Kempe, C. (eds) (1981) *Sexually Abused Children and their Families*. Oxford: Pergamon Press.

O'Hagan, K. (1989) *Working with Sexual Abuse*. Milton Keynes: Open University Press.

Olafson, E., Corwin, D. and Summit, R. (1993) 'Modern history of child sexual abuse awareness: cycles of discovery and suppression.' *Child Abuse & Neglect 17*, 1, 7–24.

Paley, J. (1997) 'Satanist abuse and alien abduction: a comparative analysis theorizing temporary lobe activity as a possible connection between anomalous memories.' *British Journal of Social Work 27*, 1, 43–70.

Parton, N. (1991) *Governing the Family: Child Care, Child Protection and the State*. Basingstoke: Macmillan.

Parton, N. (1995) 'Neglect as child protection: the political and practical outcomes.' *Children & Society 9*, 1, 67–89.

Parton, N. (1996) 'Child protection, family support and social work: a critical appraisal of the Department of Health research studies in child protection.' *Child and Family Social Work 1*, 1, 3–11.

Pelton, L. (1978) 'Child abuse and neglect: the myth of classlessness.' *American Journal of Orthopsychiatry 48*, 608–617.

Pringle, K. (1995) *Men, Masculinities and Social Welfare*. London: University College, London Press.

Pritchard, C. (1992) 'Children's homicide as an indicator of effective child protection: a comparative study of Western European statistics.' *British Journal of Social Work 22*, 6, 663–684.

Rand, D. (1993) 'Munchausen Syndrome by proxy: a complex type of emotional abuse responsible for some false allegations of child abuse in divorce.' *Issues in Child Abuse Accusations 5*, 3, 135–155.

Raynor, P. (1984) 'Evaluation with one eye closed: the empiricist agenda in social work research.' *British Journal of Social Work 14*, 1, 1–10.

Rieser, M. (1991) 'Recantation in child sexual abuse cases.' *Child Welfare 90*, 611–621.

Rist, K. (1979) 'Incest: theoretical and clinical views.' *American Journal of Orthopsychiatry 49*, 680–691.

Roberts, J. and Taylor, C. (1993) 'Sexually abused children and young people speak out.' In L. Waterhouse (ed) *Child Abuse and Child Abusers: Protection and Prevention*. London: Jessica Kingsley.

Robinson, P. (1976) *The Modernization of Sex*. London: Elek.

Rush, F. (1980) *The Best Kept Secret: Sexual Abuse of Children*. Englewood Cliffs, New Jersey: Prentice-Hall.

Russell, D. (1984) 'The prevalence and seriousness of incestuous abuse: stepfathers vs. biological fathers.' *Child Abuse & Neglect 8*, 1, 15–22.

Russell, D. (1986) *The Secret Trauma: Incest in the Lives of Girls and Women*. New York: Basic Books.

Sainsbury, E. (1989) 'Participation and paternalism.' In S. Shardlow (ed) *The Values of Change in Social Work*. London: Routledge.

Schechter, M. and Roberge, L. (1976) 'Sexual exploitation.' In R. Helfer and C. Kempe (eds) *Child Abuse and Neglect: The Family and the Community*. Cambridge, Mass.: Ballinger.

Schreier, H. (1996) 'Repeated false allegations of sexual abuse presenting to sheriffs; when is it Munchausen by Proxy?' *Child Abuse & Neglect 20*, 10, 985–991.

Schuman, J. and Galvez, M. (1996) 'A meta/multi-discursive reading of "False Memory Syndrome".' *Feminism and Psychology 6*, 1, 7–29.

Sellick, C. and Thoburn, J. (1996) *What Works in Family Placement.* Barkingside: Barnardos.

Sharland, E., Seal, H., Croucher, M., Aldgate, J. and Jones, D. (1996) *Professional Intervention in Child Sexual Abuse.* London: HMSO.

Sheldon, B. (1986) 'Social work effectiveness experiments: review and implications.' *British Journal of Social Work 16*, 2, 223–242

Smith, C. (1997) 'Children's rights: have carers abandoned values?' *Children & Society 11*, 1, 3–15.

Social Services Inspectorate (1994) *The Child, the Court and the Video: A Study of the Implementation of the Memorandum of Good Practice on Video Interviewing of Child Witnesses.* London: Department of Health.

Stace, C. (1987) *Oedipus, Sophocles.* Birmingham: Oberon Press.

Stevenson, O. (1996) 'Emotional abuse and neglect: a time for reappraisal.' *Child and Family Social Work 1*, 1, 13–18.

Stewart, K. (1996) 'Sexual abuse as a moral event.' *British Journal of Social Work 26*, 4, 493–508.

Summit, R. and Kryso, J. (1978) 'Sexual abuse of children: a clinical spectrum.' *American Journal of Orthopsychiatry 48*, 237–251.

Sydie, R. (1987) *Natural Women, Cultured Men.* Milton Keynes: Open University Press.

Thoburn, J., Lewis, A. and Shemmings, D. (1995) *Paternalism or Partnership? Family Involvement in the Child Protection Process.* London: HMSO.

Truesdell, D., Mcneil, J. and Deschner, J. (1986) 'Incidence of wife abuse in incestuous families.' *Social Work 31*, 2, 138–140.

Tunstill, J. (1997) 'Implementing the family support clauses of the 1989 Children Act: legislative, professional and organisational obstacles.' In N. Parton (ed) *Child Protection and Family Support: Tensions, Contradictions and Possibilities.* London: Routledge.

Vizard, E., Monck, E. and Misch, P. (1995) 'Child and adolescent sex abuse perpetrators: a review of the research literature.' *Journal of Child Psychology and Psychiatry 36*, 5, 731–756.

Walton, M. (1993) 'Regulation in child protection – policy failure?' *British Journal of Social Work 23*, 2, 139–156.

Waterhouse, L. and Carnie, J. (1992) 'Assessing child protection risk.' *British Journal of Social Work 22*, 1, 47–60.

Waterhouse, L., Dobash, R. and Carnie, J. (1994) *Child Sexual Abusers.* Edinburgh: Central Research Unit, Scottish Office.

Wattam, C. (1992) *Making a Case in Child Protection.* Harlow: Longman.

Wattam, C. (1997) 'Is the criminalisation of child harm and injury in the interests of the child?' *Children & Society 11*, 2, 97–107.

Weeks, J. (1989) *Sex. Politics and Society: The Regulation of Sexuality since 1800.* Harlow: Longman.

Weeks, J. (1995) *Invented Moralities: Sexual Values in an Age of Uncertainty.* Cambridge: Polity Press.

West, D. (1987) *Sexual Crimes and Confrontations: A Study of Victims and Offenders.* Gower: Aldershot.

Westcott, H. (1993) *Abuse of Children and Adults with Disabilities.* London: NSPCC.

Wiedemann, T. (1989) *Adults and Children in the Roman Empire.* London: Routledge.

Wild, N. (1986) 'Sexual abuse of children in Leeds.' *British Medical Journal 292*, 1113–1116.

Wohl, A. (1978) 'Sex and the single room: incest among the Victorian working classes.' In A. Wohl (ed) *The Victorian Family.* London: Croom Helm.

Wyre, R. (1987) *Working with Sex Offenders.* Oxford: Perry Publications.

Subject Index

Author Index